The Kindness Habit

Riverbank Books © 2016

The Kindness Habit: Transforming our Relationship to
Addictive Behaviours

Christopher Dines and Dr Barbara Mariposa
© Copyright 2016

Proofread by Lizzie Ferrar
Cover design by Danny Kent

Contact: riverbankbooksuk@gmail.com

Printed in England, United Kingdom

ISBN: 978-1-5262-0285-7

The Kindness Habit

Transforming our Relationship to
Addictive Behaviours

Christopher Dines
with
Dr Barbara Mariposa

TABLE OF CONTENTS

Dr Barbara Mariposa's acknowledgements

I am deeply indebted to Christopher Dines for approaching me, a total stranger, out of the blue in 2014. Had he not had the courage and openness to do this, we would not have been able to write this book. On meeting Christopher for the first time, it was instantly clear to me that we shared the same deep concern for, and commitment to, doing what we can to reduce human suffering. Writing the book with him was like floating down a river. Water flows around obstacles, finds its way through choppy passages and keeps on going to its destination with ease and grace. He has an ability to bring humility and openness that allows solutions and creativity to emerge. He also has a steadfastness of intention that keeps any project on track.

My family is my rock. They keep me sane and grounded. I can never thank them enough. It was because of my three beautiful daughters that I was determined to move forward from the very troubled past we shared and heal myself. When I had no connection to my own motivation, it was for them I was determined to be well.

There are many people around the world who thank John Bradshaw for the work he continues to do despite being in his eighties. What a wonderful inspiration to all of us to do what we feel passionate about, give our all to making a difference in the world, and be truthful about who we are. Thank you John Bradshaw for the putting the time and energy into reading our unpolished manuscript and for your endorsement by writing the foreword.

Thank you, reader, for being willing to open your mind and your heart and read this book. Every drop of water in the ocean makes the whole, and every shift in consciousness that each of us creates when we determine to be kinder, more generous, appreciative or honest moves the world in the right direction.

Christopher Dines' acknowledgements

I would like to thank Barbara for accepting my invitation to co-author this book. Her courage and drive reveal why she is an all-around accomplished human being. She made it easy to co-author *The Kindness Habit*. It was truly an enjoyable adventure writing and exchanging ideas. It's almost as though the book wrote itself.

Dr Barbara made it very easy for me to talk openly about addiction and my own personal experience of recovery. She has assisted many people in enhancing mental, emotional, spiritual and physical wellbeing and it has been a privilege to co-author with her.

Thank you to my loving partner, Mary McGahan, for looking over my writing and giving me positive feedback. Your wisdom and kindness is greatly appreciated.

I am very grateful to Karen Black at the John Bradshaw Media Group in Houston, Texas; thank for your kindness and assistance. Thank you so much to John Bradshaw for taking the time to read the manuscript and write a warm and inspiring foreword. You've assisted millions of people recover from addiction, dysfunctional families and 'inner child' wounds, which is truly inspiring. Your classic book, *Home Coming*, took my recovery to a whole new level!

Thank you to my business mentor, James Alexander, for your encouragement and sharing hours of experience. Your forty years of corporate business and non-profit experience and acute understanding of addiction has helped me tremendously over the last two years (especially during periods of uncertainty).

Thank you to Eileen Rockefeller Growald for your kindness and encouragement during very uncertain times. Two months after your feedback, I met Dr Barbara and the rest is history. Your courage to write and speak out so openly about your humanness helped me to finally open up and write about addiction in this book. Meeting you and Paul was a privilege. I wish you both the very best.

Thank you to Michael J. McEvoy for being a steady friend for over twelve years and for continuing to have a positive impact on my life.

You walk the walk! I wish you and your family happiness and wellbeing.

Thank you to my family and friends all over the world in recovery and for helping me through difficult times. I have great respect and appreciation for the twelve-step fellowships, therapists, counsellors and addiction rehab treatment centres – you all keep the recovery movement strong, fresh and vibrant in the United Kingdom and all over the world. I appreciate my spiritual teachers who walked me through the painstaking process of rebuilding a new and wonderful life free from drugs, alcohol and destructive addictive patterns of behaviour. And finally, thank you to the reader. I hope you gain value from *The Kindness Habit*.

FOREWORD

By John E. Bradshaw, Sr.

The Kindness Habit is the fruit of two very kind and courageous people. Reading it is therapeutic; I welcome this book with open arms and gratitude. I have been lecturing on and writing about 'addictiveness' as the root of any addiction for many years. Now I have a book to recommend that illuminates the meaning and dynamics of 'addictiveness'.

Christopher Dines and Dr Barbara Mariposa reframe the whole concept of addictions in a positive way, seeing them as false friends. Our addictions seem like the best solution available to us at the time, because our consciousness has been limited by our shame-based self. Once we realise this, we can be more gentle and 'kind' to ourselves.

Addictiveness is rooted in toxic shame. Shame is a natural affect. It exists to help us form our early sense of identity; it guides us to form a conscience and a sense of guilt (moral shame).

Without the effect of shame, the foundation for our moral life would collapse. As the philosopher Nietzsche said long ago, "Everybody needs a sense of shame, but nobody needs to be ashamed."

Being ashamed happens because few of us escape from the dogmatic and patriarchal religious systems we were born into. I grew up believing that I was loveable only when I was not being myself. Dogmatic patriarchal systems measure us by their narrow and rigid dogmatic rules. We are told what to think and not to think, what to feel and what not to feel, and what to desire and what is forbidden to desire. To fail to measure up to these rules (which none of us can because they violate our true self) is what transforms natural shame (healthy) into a shame-based self – a self against itself.

The feeling of shame is transformed into a flawed identity, the sense that, in my very being, I am flawed and defective. I've called this the hole in our soul. The 'hole' in our soul is like a black hole that sucks up anything in its path. Toxic, absolutised shame is a 'being wound'. As such, it feels hopeless. Toxic shame forces us into hiding and the fear of exposure. And since our thoughts, feelings, needs and wants have been repressed, we don't know who we are, what we think, feel or want.

The only way out of the hopelessness caused by our toxic shame is with an addiction. And as Christopher and Dr Barbara point out, when one addiction fails, we move to another one. We don't have an addiction; we ARE ensconced in 'addictiveness'.

The authors of *The Kindness Habit* show us that the sure way out is to become vulnerable. We do this by coming out of hiding and by entering into dialogue with another person, by letting them see us in our wounded, shame-based self. The moment I walked into a twelve-step meeting and said, "I'm John, I am an alcoholic", my shame was reduced and I began the journey of healing my wounded self – which is the core of my 'addictiveness', the repressed energy that creates the 'hole' in my soul.

I continued to stay off of alcohol (fifty years sober) but after ten years, I began a love and sex addiction. The 'hole' in my soul was not healed. In 1981, I joined a sex and love addicts twelve-step programme. Once again, I had to come out of hiding and confess what had become a shameful lifestyle. Thanks to my Higher Power (whom I choose to call God), I ceased all sexual acting out on August 11, 1981. After joining a group of like-addicted people, I did two years of therapy to grieve my lost self and my abandonment and abuse issues.

In 1985, I went on national PBS with my first of five ten-part series. Over the next few years, I achieved a loving sense of self. I embraced myself with kindness and gave up my resentment for, and judgement of, others in a 'good enough' way.

I cannot possibly do justice to this book in this foreword. To experience the insight and true wisdom in the pages that follow, be kind to yourself and read *The Kindness Habit*.

John E. Bradshaw, Sr.
Three times #1 *New York Times* bestseller
Senior Fellow at The Meadows Treatment Center

INTRODUCTION

How this book came into being

Dr Barbara Mariposa's view

We are all addicts in one way or another. Stuck in habits that don't serve us and reacting with patterns of behaviour that don't reflect our true worth and that have potentially damaging consequences to ourselves and/or others.

When people speak of addiction, what usually springs to mind is what's called 'substance addiction': the habitual ingestion of some material or other that might make us temporarily feel good, but also has the quality of making us crave it more and more, of getting us hooked. Sometimes to the point where we can't live without it, even though we know it's damaging us. Things like nicotine, cocaine, heroin, alcohol. Even sugar. Most people with a classic substance addiction will often strongly deny that this is the case.

Then there's process addiction. Some form of behaviour that we are compelled to engage in that, again, has an element of self-destruction in it. Like gambling, overeating, undereating, pulling out hair, abusive relationships.

In this book, we're going to ask some questions about addictions. How come we seek refuge in forms of behaviour that don't serve us? And, more importantly, what can we do about that? How can we transform our relationship to our self and our habits in order to have choice and freedom and be at peace on the inside?

What are the ingredients of a life where we can find that sense of release or refuge within ourselves, rather than having to turn to external, damaging substances and behaviours? Or whatever your 'thing' is.

We also want to shift the conversation around addiction. Rather than seeing the 'thing', the addiction, as the enemy, the evil element that is ruining your life, let's see how to shift the approach to one that we strongly believe works better. How can you transform your relationship to the 'thing' and to yourself so that you find lasting inner strength and no longer need to find false refuge in self-abusive habits?

An important first step in this process is to recognise that your 'thing' has served a useful purpose. It has been part of how you protect yourself, what you do to soothe, assuage, and quieten some inner turmoil. A place to go to find some peace, without which you would not function well on a day-to-day basis. Like a friend. Your 'thing' has become like a friend. A place of refuge.

We all do it. Act in ways that don't serve us. Protect ourselves. When we feel under threat, we act to protect ourselves. It's a survival thing.

The possibility that presents itself is to find other 'friends' that don't damage us. To connect with something deeper inside ourselves that is always there and never broken. To step beyond the fear that keeps us stuck. To realise our potential for growth, self-care and self-compassion.

That's what this book is about. We sincerely trust that, wherever you are in your life, it will inspire you to move forward, in the light of what is possible, and find refuge inside yourself rather than in your 'thing'.

A note about meeting Christopher. One day, I received an email from a complete stranger in my inbox, inviting me to co-author a book. Not something that happens every day.

My initial reaction was one of slight suspicion. So I ignored it. But there was something in the tone that lingered (you know how even an inert email can seem to have an underlying tone!). So I replied some days later. We agreed to speak on the phone. Christopher's voice exuded a strength, humility and calm.

We agreed to meet. In the hotel café sat a beaming beacon of warmth and gentleness. In our initial conversation, we explored writing a book together and quickly settled on the subject of addictions, agreeing that if we could shift the conversation around this important subject, there was a huge potential to make a difference in a massive yet hidden subject surrounded with shame and guilt. Shame and guilt that perpetuate the need for secrecy and denial.

First job? To shift that context of shame and guilt to allow truth and gentleness, compassion and healing, hope and honesty.

On my own journey, shame and guilt are states I have had to battle with – a deep down feeling that, somehow or other, being me was not okay. I've always been a bit of an outsider, and felt 'different', like I didn't fit in. The constant chatter in my head has centred on themes of inadequacy, failure, and self-doubt. I used to dread meeting people in case I couldn't think of anything to say. Everyone else seemed so confident, so at ease with themselves, an ease I longed to acquire but had no idea where to start.

I guess this led to me being deeply fascinated by what goes on in other people's heads, and a heartfelt desire to find ways to achieve peace, both for myself and for others. I soon realised that I was not alone in my internal sense of 'dis-ease', and began to explore the connection between our thoughts and feelings and our physical health.

I've made a lot of mistakes along the way, and paradoxically as it may seem, I can now say that it's these mistakes that have led me to find answers, answers that are not new but seem to have a universal, timeless truth to them.

This is not a 'how-to' book, or a scientific book. However, we sincerely hope that what you read helps you take steps forward, wherever you are in your journey.

Christopher Dines' view

I came across an exceptional talk online. The speaker was Dr Barbara Mariposa, medical doctor and wellness pioneer. It was refreshing to hear another human being speak so openly about facing harrowing circumstances and coming through them with grace and equanimity. Barbara shared her life story in an open and honest fashion.

We were both running courses on mindfulness and emotional intelligence and so, after speaking to my partner, I decided to contact her to see if we could collaborate in some way. And so I sent her a short email and asked if she would be interested in co-authoring a book that could assist many people.

I have to say, I felt terribly nervous before meeting her and I started to doubt what value I could bring to the table. Up until that point, I had felt utterly confident in my ability to teach and write. After all, I had five books published and had led successful workshops and seminars since my early twenties and, prior to that, created a successful DJ career in the electronic dance music industry from scratch.

However, Barbara is an exceptionally experienced medical doctor (many years of practical experience in the service of others) and an exceptional one at that; she has been practising Zen for decades and is very active in the mindfulness scene. Thoughts were racing: "Who am I to co-author with a high-grade medical doctor?", "She has a super high intellect and I didn't finish high school", "You'll be exposed as being inferior if you attempt to work with her", etc.

Thankfully, due to practising mindfulness, I knew that my old toxic mental monologues (unhelpful thoughts) didn't have to dominate my actions. However, I decided to talk to my mentor and shared my insecurities with him. He listened very carefully and reminded me that I had genuine experience with respect to assisting people address addictiveness and mentoring professionals to be mindful and emotionally intelligent.

I decided to turn up with a positive mental attitude and let go of the outcome; what will be, will be.

As a result of the meeting and a lengthy correspondence, we realised that we had a shared concern with respect to the rise of addictions and the many unhappy people in society. In a lot of cases, untreated addiction can be fatal. However, for many people who are substance misusers or process users, tremendous suffering and family dysfunction become 'the norm'.

We discussed the great value of recovery, mindfulness, self-awareness, gratitude, self-compassion, emotional intelligence, meditation, emotional wellbeing, forgiveness, success, living with an open heart and creating healthy relationships with ourselves and our fellow human beings. This fascinating conversation inspired us to co-write this book, *The Kindness Habit*.

I have learnt that if we develop wholesome relationships, life becomes far more fulfilling and enjoyable – we begin to feel a sense of belonging. Conversely, if we do not have healthy relationships, our reality becomes dysfunctional, addictive and destructive. The most important relationship, however, is with ourselves.

Sadly, many relationships are governed by an addiction of being 'outcome-orientated'. The desire to fix unresolved childhood emotional trauma and suppressed grief is so intense that rather than going deep within our hearts to start the process of healing, we look to 'fix' ourselves by using a 'thing' or a 'substance' or a 'person' until we realise that they cannot fulfil us, therefore creating even more suffering and a yearning to be loved.

I've learnt through my own personal journey that no one can fill the empty void inside – I had to bring out my authentic self (inner child), my Higher Power and reconnect with my heart and spirit with the aid of fellowship and people on a spiritual path. I learnt to direct love and kindness inwards before I could truly be kind and loving towards others.

Tragically, because many addicts are not given sufficient love, nurturing and non-shaming dialogue at crucial stages in their early emotional development, they are on a quest to find contentment from a source outside of themselves.

Their parents might have provided bountifully for them; however, their parents were never fully emotionally present while parenting, which made their children feel starved of emotional nourishment.

Some addicts do not even have basic parenting and instead are beaten, sexually abused, left to be looked after by a dysfunctional 'carer', put in orphan homes or rejected by their community. If you calculate the millions of emotionally neglected children and observe them growing up together trying to 'get by in life', you will understand why many adults (adult children) have addictive personalities.

Regardless of the different stages in our human development, unless we learn how to create loving and fulfilling relationships (with ourselves and others), addiction will follow – not necessarily as a manifestation of substance misuse but in the form of codependence, compulsive thinking, unhealthy relationships, sex and love addictions, overeating, insidious incarnations of self-harm and so on.

Dr Barbara Mariposa and I have framed this book in the simplest way: through a friendly, practical and compassionate dialogue. The questions asked are inspired by genuine enquiries that have been presented to us during workshops, classes and retreats. The purpose of co-writing this book is to bring clarity to the reader and help answer the many challenges that people have with respect to addictiveness, recovery and authentic fulfilment.

CHAPTER ONE

A close encounter of the unexpected kind

I was sitting at a bar the other night with some friends when this guy came up to order a drink. He was a bit the worse for wear but smartly dressed – affluent, well spoken and well mannered. What he said nearly knocked me off my stool. He started to talk really openly about his addiction: to cocaine (doing it for years, apparently). No nasal septum. He looked so respectable and normal.

Dr Barbara: That's interesting. Most people have a stereotypical image of addicts as being a particular kind of person. But the truth is addicts are often highly functioning, successful people: city types, bankers, lawyers, doctors. It's estimated about fifteen per cent of doctors are addicted to something.

Wow. That's incredible!

Christopher: Scores of high-powered men and women are addicted to substances or destructive addictive patterns of behaviour. As a matter of fact, it is easier to hide one's addiction while maintaining a high-powered position compared to the addicts and alcoholics we see sleeping on street corners.

I always thought that it was just dropouts, celebrities or heroin addicts who had a problem. So addiction is much more wide-spread than I imagined?

Dr Barbara: As a nation (in the United Kingdom), addiction costs about sixty million pounds a year in lost productivity. That's a lot. And mostly, it's a hidden problem. So that guy in the bar was really special in being so open about it. What happened next?

While the guy was knocking back shots of rum, he talked freely about how he had lost touch with himself, lost his way. Got submerged in a world of denial and lies and how it all happened without him really noticing. Like it just crept up on him, and then BOOM, ten years later, realising having no nasal septum was the least of his problems. He became paranoid and sometimes felt suicidal.

Dr Barbara: What did you say?

I was just listening. I couldn't believe what I was hearing. It made me think though.

Dr Barbara: Yeah? What about?

Well, it made me wonder about myself and my own behaviour. I mean, none of us is perfect, are we?

Christopher: We all make mistakes, and I certainly have my blind spots.

I just feel that something in me is not quite right. I feel like something is missing and I can't quite figure it out.

Dr Barbara: I get what you're saying. Like we're all carrying some kind of secret inside us. Something we don't want anyone to know about. Something we're ashamed of.

Yes, I guess so. I don't mean to be reserved – it's just that the stranger I met in the bar triggered something within me and I'm starting to question things.

Christopher: We suffer when we suppress what's on our mind; we pretend we're fine when we're terrified. This causes great pain: a feeling of loneliness. The fact that you can identify your internal reservations is a good start.

I can relate to loneliness and suffering. That's for sure!

Dr Barbara: Imagine what it would be like if it was okay to talk about all these things in an open way, without having to worry about what others might think – if it was possible to heal the sense of toxic shame and guilt. Given that a lot of addicts are people in positions of authority, that could make quite an impact on our society.

How do we do that? Open up and talk freely, I mean?

Dr Barbara: That, my friend, is a really good question. And one we're going to explore. I can get a sense of a world where, instead of making decisions from a place of inadequacy and survival, we are able to make choices that really serve us, those around us, and the world in general. From a place of feeling at peace with ourselves. Imagine what that would be like. What do you think, Christopher?

Christopher: Exactly. To be open and honest in a non-shaming environment plays a huge role in assisting us to heal from toxic shame and guilt. It's our secrets and isolation that perpetuate addiction. Can you relate to that?

I do have a tendency to bottle things up. My family brought me up to never ever discuss my feelings or fears; otherwise, it would make me appear weak and cowardly. Talking to you about addiction doesn't feel comfortable.

Christopher: Lots of us have been conditioned to keep a stiff upper lip: "Don't talk, don't trust and don't feel." The thing is, suppressing our fears makes it almost impossible to address them. To a certain extent, we're all afraid, and shy away from being exposed.

Hmm ... I don't mean to digress, but how come a guy like that in the bar got into that kind of mess in the first place? How on earth does a high-performance person end up feeling hopeless? That left me flabbergasted.

Dr Barbara: Yes, let's look at it from the beginning. I've had my own personal experience of addictive behaviour and breakdown, so I hope I can offer something useful here.

What addictive behaviour did you suffer from? Have you stopped now? I would feel a lot more comfortable if the two of you opened up before I continue.

Dr Barbara: I married twice, to men who were completely unsuitable to the person I am. In order to hide my own feelings of emptiness, I became addicted to helping others. This also allowed me to hide an unhealthy relationship to food. As a teenager, it seemed that as I got slimmer, I became more attractive, more socially acceptable. I got hooked in a preoccupation with weight control. When my second marriage to a violent alcoholic broke down, this addictive personality popped up again and I drank heavily. It was the addiction to self-abuse in my second marriage that nearly killed me, literally.

Wow. I wasn't expecting that answer. What about you, Christopher?

Christopher: Drug and alcohol addiction almost killed me. I was a grave substance misuser in my teens. I started drinking at ten, smoking at eleven and by the time I attended high school aged twelve, I was regularly smoking marijuana and drinking alcohol on weekends. I was a full-blown alcoholic at thirteen. Tragically, I had my stomach pumped at fourteen and although I promised my family I would never drink again, I started less than two weeks later. I was completely hooked on alcohol.

Then what happened?

Christopher: By the time I was fifteen, I started using ecstasy and cocaine. Life started to become very dark after I crossed that line. By the time I was nineteen, I started attending support groups. However, the addictive patterns of behaviour still had awesome momentum, and it took another two years before I finally hit a dark rock bottom. I stopped using drugs and alcohol less than two weeks after my twenty-first birthday and since then, I haven't used a mind- or mood-altering substance. That was close to twelve years ago.

That's a big deal. I'm very curious as to how the two of you have addressed your addictions. I feel a bit more relaxed now to open up, but don't expect me to be as candid as the two of you. So what caused your addiction?

Christopher: Addiction (addictiveness) is a process, like anything else in the physical universe. It's very complex to precisely point out what exactly caused me to become addicted to substances, although there are many theories. One thing I know is that I was terrified of reality. To be sober back then (without a sufficient recovery programme) meant to feel raw and exposed all of the time; the childhood trauma, hurt and abuse damaged my coping skills. Internally, I was mentally, emotionally and spiritually isolated. Thus, the process of addiction is a sad and lonely existence. I felt incredibly lonely while in active addiction.

So addictions are a symptom of seeking and craving?

Dr Barbara: Let's explore the whole addictions thing a bit more. Usually, people think of addiction as drugs: a product or 'thing' that we have to have to survive. That's called substance addiction. We can include in this category cocaine, heroin, nicotine, even caffeine and sugar. The criterion is that we crave the substance when we don't have it, even though we know it does us no good. And we need more and more of it to produce the same desired effect. Often, the mind will deny that there are damaging effects in order to justify seeking it out.

That sounds like an awful cycle.

Christopher: By and large, people who are seriously addicted to mind- and mood-altering substances feel terribly awkward unless they are masking reality with numbness or oblivion. I felt so exposed and ashamed if I didn't have some sort of mind-altering substance in my system. The mind of an addict is so restless and the sense of loneliness is so profound that the only rational thing is to self-medicate. If you were to ask a drug addict or an alcoholic to be honest and ask them why they use substances (even at the risk of dying and causing suffering to loved ones), more often than not, they will say they use drugs for medicinal purposes.

I can feel exposed a lot of the time for no apparent reason. It's a horrible feeling. What about gambling and shopping addictions? Do they feel the same as the cocaine addict I met in the bar?

Christopher: Yes, addiction can manifest in all sorts of ways. The internal loneliness and yearning to search for something to fulfil themselves is essentially the same. Addiction takes many forms. Whether someone is addicted to a substance or harmful behaviour, it's the internal silent suffering that lies beneath addictive behaviour.

So it's like a vicious, lonely cycle?

Christopher: Yes, it is a vicious cycle. They feel uptight, restless and overwhelmingly lonely, and so they seek a solution: a substance, compulsive shopping sprees, sex, pornography, controlling others, overeating, gambling, etc. Then once they realise that the 'fix' hasn't fulfilled them (and has caused them more damage), the feelings of guilt, toxic shame, remorse and regret kick in.

The emphasis on loneliness, toxic shame and isolation is really hitting a nerve. Do we know anything about the mechanisms that keep us stuck? How does this all work in the brain?

Dr Barbara: An important thing to realise is that after a certain amount of repetition, any cycle of behaviour is etched out in the neural pathways in the brain. Every action or thought pattern that's repeated regularly wires itself into the substance of the brain. The brain changes shape according to how you use it. That's how habits become habits. One nerve cell connects with another and then another. When this pattern of connection is repeated often enough, the nerve cells (or neurons) learn what's coming next, causing one to fire off automatically, which causes the rest of the network to fire off.

Go on… This is fascinating.

Dr Barbara: In reality, we're talking about hundreds of millions of connections in each pathway, not single neurons. But the principle is the same. In a piece of brain tissue the size of a grain of sand, there are sixty-four million neural connections! The point I want to underline here is that when we understand that the brain is a living, transforming, malleable organ in the body, we can see that it's possible to create new neural pathways. We can overcome conditioned responses and learn new ways of thinking, behaving and relating to ourselves that will alter the substrate of the brain. In other words, there is hope. A lot of hope. With the right guidance, intention and knowledge, everyone can move beyond their addictive behaviours and thought patterns.

That's amazing! So if I were to admit to you at some point that I might have a problem with some type of addiction, then there is hope? Really?

Christopher: Yes, really!

Dr Barbara: Realising and admitting that you have a problem is a crucial first step.

This guy at the bar talked about the extreme lengths to which he would go to get cocaine. How it ruined friendships and relationships. He became an inveterate liar. At some level, he was justifying it all and completely blind to it. The longer the night went on, the more frequently he visited the gentleman's room (which I suspect was to use cocaine) and the more he drank like a fish. By the time I left, he couldn't look me in the eye.

Dr Barbara: He had enormous courage to face himself. I have so much respect for him.

Christopher: To admit his addiction is a massive step and if you feel that you can do the same, even better. I just hope he can still admit he has a problem when he has dried up.

That makes sense. I realise I'm not judging him. I'm actually a bit grateful. He's provoked me into taking a look at my own behaviour.

Dr Barbara: Let's remember that, at some level, most of us could say that we do things that are not necessarily good for us and can't stop, even though we feel we should stop. Like shopping and spending money to get that short-lived 'retail therapy buzz', or eating when we're not hungry. These kinds of things represent another form of addiction, which is called process addiction. Gambling is an example of this and the bingeing and purging of bulimia. We're not hooked on a chemical but hooked on a repetitive form of behaviour. Addiction to digital devices is the new twenty-first century one.

If you put it like that, are any of us not addicts?

Dr Barbara: Indeed. That's a really good point. Let's take a closer look at that. Some people are addicted to perfectionism. They can't accept their flaws, human mistakes, the natural cycle of learning and growth that feeds off making mistakes and being okay with that. They are extraordinarily self-critical and driven, which, it has to be said, makes them excellent cogs in the corporate work machine. The personal cost is huge though.

After listening to what you have both said on addiction, I feel that I might have a problem. I think I'm hooked on destructive relationships. I can relate to 'retail therapy' and eating to mask pain but toxic relationships are causing me so much pain.

Christopher: Do you mean you find yourself attracted to partners who are not emotionally available and seeking to control people in relationships?

Yes. That's it! I always try to have relationships with partners who cannot emotionally commit and who are also acting out through harmful behaviour. Most of my personal relationships are not good for me. I don't really have any 'real' friends. I feel so ashamed and stupid about this.

Christopher: That is a massive breakthrough. It takes courage to get in touch with your emotions and to tell your truth.

Thanks. I just wish I felt courageous. Instead, I feel terribly vulnerable.

Christopher: Being vulnerable is okay for now. It takes bravery to open up and share. Bear in mind, relationships are the cradle of humanity and they can be wholesome and fulfilling or they can be addictive and destructive.

Dr Barbara: And they can be anywhere along that spectrum, at different points in time. When we're under stress, our 'default setting' behaviours tend to kick in. You know that expression 'it brings out the worst in me'? When you're with someone and neither of you is particularly at peace with themselves, then it is more likely that you're both playing out old scripts, ways of behaving that are defensive, fear-based, and driven by survival patterns. Then it can be difficult to find space for any real and honest communication.

I recognise that this is often what's happening. There's no real communication.

Dr Barbara: Exactly. It happens even in closer relationships. Our habit-driven self will lead us to choose partners whose default setting neatly dovetails into our own. Then they lock into place and we're stuck. It's so great that you are examining your pattern in relationships this way. If you can start to see the underlying mechanism and its automaticity, you can start to make different choices. And becoming free of addictive behaviour depends on the ability to make choices rather than operate on autopilot.

CHAPTER TWO

Why me?

Autopilot, hmm. That makes me think that maybe I'm on autopilot in relationships. I wonder if I'm suffering in my relationships, or rather the lack of them, because of some kind of addictive behaviour?

Christopher: If we are continuing to attract partners that are emotionally unavailable, then it's essential that we observe our own addictive patterns rather than focusing on theirs.

Why? What are you getting at?

Christopher: Because we can only really change ourselves. We cannot change anyone else.

Dr Barbara: This is so true. It's about taking responsibility for where we are in our lives. As long as we focus on the other person, we can't move forward in ourselves. In a way, discovering the power of taking personal responsibility is the first step on the road to freedom.

I'm sorry, but I'm finding this a bit hard to take. Are you suggesting that I'm always to blame? All I want to know is why I'm suffering.

Dr Barbara: It's so great that you can identify that that's the feeling that comes up for you around this topic. Let that feeling be. Just be present to it. And the thoughts that surround it, keeping the feeling in place – just let them be. All thoughts and feelings are represented by electrochemical activity in the brain. This activity subsides naturally if we let it. So be kind to yourself and realise that you noticed how you were feeling rather than getting sucked into it. Let it pass. This is the nature of things. All things pass, a bit like the weather.

I'll try to let these 'feelings' pass, but I'm starting to feel ashamed. I hate being blamed for things.

Christopher: No one here is 'blaming' you. If we are constantly attracting destructive relationships or indulging in sexual or emotional intrigue or codependent patterns, then it might be worth assessing the choices that led us to people who are emotionally unavailable, that's all.

So am I to blame?

Dr Barbara: Blame and guilt are habitual ways of thinking and feeling that drive addiction. We learn these patterns early on in life. What we're saying here is that, in order to heal, we need to step outside of blame, guilt, shame, and self-loathing. These are not helpful concepts. It's nobody's fault, least of all yours. We're not playing that blame game here. The name of the game is: find a place inside yourself that lies beyond these stereotypical patterns. One of the most important things I had to learn was how to find a place of kindness and compassion inside myself. A place where we can get in touch with our inherent goodness. Nothing can destroy that. Just by thinking about our inherent goodness and stretching our imagination in the direction of self-acceptance and kindness, you are already altering the wiring in your brain.

Rationally, that makes sense to me, but I'm feeling a wave of self-doubt.

Dr Barbara: Maybe a voice inside you says, "What nonsense. I don't have that kind of goodness inside of me." That's just your patterns, your autopilot reaction to the new idea we're giving you in order to defend or protect yourself. See if you can move your attention towards creating this awareness though, the sense that you are inherently good. Do this whenever you notice thoughts and feelings of blame, guilt and shame arise. Move your attention intentionally towards creating a sense of your own goodness. Practise this when you feel okay. It's like building a new muscle. It takes practice. The more in touch with this space inside ourselves we are, the more we discover the ability to make wise, wholesome choices.

Okay then. Logically, that makes sense but it's still hurting my pride. I've always prided myself on making good choices in my professional life. The idea of being incompetent in this area eats away at me.

Dr Barbara: Oh, I know that one! My version is: "How could a super-educated, intelligent, creative, powerful, independent woman like me possibly be so incompetent in her choice of partners?"

Well, I'm glad I'm not the only one.

Christopher: I also used to attract unsuitable partners who created immense drama. And then, one day, I had to come to terms with the fact that they were not the problem. After all, what was it about me that continued to attract emotionally unavailable women? What was it about me that attracted many fair-weather friends and abusive people? That question led to a long process of healing to find wellbeing.

I can relate to all of that. Most of my 'friends' are people I have used to further my career. My family motto is 'use people for their strengths'.

Christopher: Let's not forget the cocaine addict you met in the bar who was a highly competent professional. He was probably paid to make sound professional choices. But the decisions he made in his personal life were questionable.

Yeah, I guess so.

Dr Barbara: In a way, it's reassuring that you can see that you make good choices in your professional life. Then you know that you have that capacity intact. How interesting it would be if you were to apply the same skills to handling yourself. It's a great step you've taken to talk about your damaging patterns. I hope you can see that, and congratulate yourself. Naturally, it might make you feel a little vulnerable and that's not a familiar place to be for a lot of people.

We spend so much time and energy proving to the world how 'together' we are, how strong and okay we are. That's the mask we wear to protect ourselves.

I have a lot of masks I present to different people. I'm often called a chameleon by my co-workers. I feel like I have to be one in order to survive in my industry. It's a tough field to work in.

Dr Barbara: Given the amount of hostility there is in some work environments, it's completely understandable. But our real strength lies in our vulnerability. That sounds paradoxical, but when we are able to stand tall in the face of our apparent weaknesses, we have indeed become a fuller person. We have moved closer to the person we are, whole and complete, loved and loving, courageous and compassionate.

I'm sorry if I was a bit defensive. This isn't easy, openly admitting my 'stuff' but somehow it seems easier to do this with a couple of relative strangers.

Christopher: No problem. I often reflect on a quote from the 14th Dalai Lama, which I find helpful: "Being aware of a single shortcoming within yourself is far more useful than being aware of a thousand in someone else."

Again, that is morally brilliant, but it's extremely hard to do.

Dr Barbara: Yes, you are so right! It certainly seems that way. But think about it a little more. How much energy and effort goes into keeping up appearances, covering up our feelings, and living with the image we generate to cover up our habits? What you have done in this conversation is open up, say what is there to be said, even when it felt a little uncomfortable, and allowed things to unfold. What it took was staying in the present, being aware, and focusing on what's happening now. The seeming paradox is that when we do this, growth is inevitable.

I hope so. I'm afraid of being stuck in my addiction, but at least it's familiar to me. I don't know what will happen to me if I were to overcome my addiction. Who would I be without it?

Christopher: Remaining static in active addiction is harder than a gentle self-appraisal. The addictive mind, however, will convince us that to create new and healthy habits and to do our original pain work is harder than repeating self-perpetuating, destructive behaviour. Surely it's much harder living with toxic shame, self-hatred and guilt than making a few adjustments in our habits?

Yes, but I don't want to be some 'saintly' figure. It all seems a bit self-righteous or religious. All this talk of inner goodness. How would that go down at work?

Dr Barbara: I get that. And this is not a religious business. This is a human business. How to succeed at being a human. There isn't much of a roadmap for how to do this in most people's lives. Most of the roadmaps seem to have been provided by religions. But it really is about being human in a way that works, both for ourselves and for society.

Hmm, I'm not sure... But I'll bear in mind what you're saying for now...

Dr Barbara: Again, let's emphasise that we all have addictive patterns in some way. You are not being singled out here. We're discussing the human condition, what we all do in the mistaken notion that avoiding and denying our feelings is what works. We learnt it from our parents, our society, our culture.

So it's not my fault then?

Dr Barbara: It's nobody's fault. What we learn as we continue to grow as adults is how to regain that childlike awareness and curiosity about the world. We get in touch with our desire to heal. We learn to trust our innate abilities and to move beyond our limitations so we can move forward and realise that we can transform our lives, moment by moment, through choice. This is the ability to – in the middle of the path that leads to some destructive tendency – wake up, get in touch with that inherent goodness we talked about before, and choose, defying our own history and rewriting who we are.

Please, go on…

Dr Barbara: Let's imagine you're about to do something out of habit that you know isn't good for you. Imagine that you had the ability, right then and there, to slow it all down by a split second and see what was happening – just notice it all. To see the stimulus and have an awareness of what your automatic response to that stimulus would be. To be more self-aware, in other words. This is the essence of mindfulness.

I've heard of mindfulness. It's been all over the news recently. How does mindfulness help me with my addictiveness?

Dr Barbara: Practising mindfulness helps us slow down the reaction patterns that run us. We become more self-aware, more able to notice our thoughts and feelings, to realise that these are events, things that occur, not who we are. It's as if a gap opens up between the stimulus and our automatic response to it. And in that gap, as Viktor Frankl so brilliantly said, lies our freedom, the freedom to choose. And this is, as he said, the greatest freedom and maybe the only one there is. All addicts are struggling to find this freedom, as are all of the people I currently know. The problems an addict faces are the existential problems we all face. If we can, in this moment now, accept that things are exactly the way they are right now, the acceptance is like a magic key that opens up that gap.

I've never considered why I've been in so much pain until now. In fact, I didn't really know I was. I'm slowly coming to realise that my addictive nature is hiding my own suffering. It's not about anyone else or a substance. It's coming to terms with that.

Dr Barbara: What you just said is brilliant. Suffering is such a strong word in our world, seemingly so dangerous, so let's take a better look at it. In the common translation of the Buddhist texts, 'suffering' is the word most commonly used when talking about what it's like to be human. Another word we could use that might better represent what the Buddhists are talking about is 'frustration': the constant sense that things are not right and we don't know how to put them right, be that ourselves, others or the circumstances in our lives.

Oh, I know that feeling. That's what makes me go to the gym or buy a new shirt when I don't need one. It's as if I think that changing something on the outside will make me feel more at ease on the inside. It does, briefly, but it never lasts...

Dr Barbara: A lot of us live with this constant sense of "Something is wrong with the way things are right now", or "If only I could get a better job, haircut, partner, or pair of shoes, everything would be okay." All this comes from a deeper sense that "I am not okay." Some people would say that this sense of dissatisfaction is what drives us to get things done, to change things. And, to a certain extent, that might be true. Martin Luther King, Jr. was deeply dissatisfied with the racial injustices in the world and that caused him to take action. But first he had to accept the way it was, see it for what it was. This acceptance is the first step to action.

Yes, but how does acceptance relate to my own suffering?

Dr Barbara: Acceptance means understanding that things are the way they are right now. This might be "I am hungry" or "I am an addict". Once we fully understand that this is the state of affairs, we can do something about it. It's the constant denial of what is that keeps us stuck. The moment we fully accept that, in this moment, what is already is, then we have created a shift in awareness that allows us to move forward.

What about acceptance in abusive and addictive relationships? Surely I'm not expected to accept such a thing?

Dr Barbara: Acceptance doesn't mean putting up with or giving in. In an abusive relationship, it's the recognition and acceptance that this is not working for you that allows you to make other healthier choices. I know this from my own experience.

Can you share some of your experiences?

Dr Barbara: I had to go through so much pain and denial, guilt, shame and blame to recognise that I'd married an alcoholic. Beyond that, this man that I loved was abusive and was damaging me and our children both psychologically and physically. When I was finally able to wake up and accept this reality, then I was able to do something about it. I had to take responsibility for the situation I was in and move to another place inside myself, way beyond guilt, blame and shame. It took time, and it took a lot of mindful self-awareness.

How on earth did you get over that? I mean, that's incredible. How brave of you!

Dr Barbara: One of the things I did was to meditate every day and make a real effort to turn my thoughts towards forgiveness, kindness and compassion. Towards myself and towards others. This was not easy and I couldn't do it in the initial phase after the divorce. There was a lot of turbulence in the years that followed, and I was really just doing my best to survive. I was extremely unwell.

I'm sorry to hear that. At least you came through it.

Dr Barbara: The thing is that, underneath it all, what was growing was something that could not be damaged: my true sense of myself. As I got stronger, and meditation helped me enormously here, that part of me grew stronger and I made some very clear choices about how I wanted to be, what my core values were. This guided me.

That's an interesting notion – that we can literally build ourselves back up from the core values we choose.

Dr Barbara: I rewrote my own history and now see that these times of internal struggle and the naked honesty of having everything ripped away from me got me to where I am today. I began to rewire decades of neural pathways in my brain. My thought patterns and feelings towards myself circled around me being unworthy, a bad person, a failure. When we begin to see that these beliefs are just that, beliefs, not 'the truth', and that they were constructed out of events in our upbringing, we can start to see how the repetitive thoughts in our head are driven by habit. This too is an addiction! We're addicted to the notion that we're not okay.

That's so true!

Dr Barbara: There is another way of relating to ourselves, another source of identity that we create, moment by moment, by getting in touch with something deeper inside us. Call it what you will, but for me, I feel that there is some core of goodness, some essence of me that has always been there and is indestructible. My healing journey required me to get back in touch with this sense of myself.

That's so moving. Thank you for talking about all this.

Dr Barbara: The questions I have these days revolve around how we can transform the context in which we live our lives right now. Regardless of what has happened in the past, where we are now is the starting point. Acknowledging and accepting our inner turmoil allows us to start seeing things differently, now. And now is all that is attainable. The past is in the past. The future is unwritten, as Joe Strummer said. The choices we make now don't have to be driven by the past, once we can see how the past is holding and moulding us. And the choices we make now create our future. How can we increase our ability to make wise and wholesome choices?

That's a lot to take in. You have both given me a lot to digest.

Christopher: Let's pause for a moment to reflect and continue the conversation in a while. How does that sound?

Sounds good to me.

CHAPTER THREE

Another fine mess you've gotten me into, Stanley

How come a person like me, so successful in one way, ends up destroying life in another way? I understand what you said about addiction and needing to look within, rather than blaming substances or people, but I still have some doubts.

Dr Barbara: The way I see it, all our addictive behaviours are ways of avoiding what we're feeling. It's interesting. Human beings are highly social animals. We need meaningful interactions with our fellow humans to feel whole and complete. In fact, ninety percent of the wiring in the newer parts of our brains is to do with social and emotional intelligence. The development of these so-called higher faculties is what sets us apart from most other mammals. They allow for things like the development of language, abstract art, the ability to be self-aware and reflect on our own thoughts, to reflect on what others are thinking and feeling, and to develop the theory of mind.

That sounds very interesting. Please continue.

Dr Barbara: Without proper guidance and learning, this ability to reflect on ourselves can be our downfall. The mind turned on itself can wreak havoc, with self-criticism, self-doubt and self-absorption. You don't find a goat walking around a mountain path saying to itself, "Jeez, I'm so useless. Why can't I chew down on this grass faster? Look what a mess I've made of it." Or a rabbit saying to itself, "My life is such a mess. Look at her over there. She's so much fluffier than me. Maybe I should get a fluff transplant." As humans, so much of our thinking is self-destructive. Our capacity for self-reflection can turn on us. How many of us are, in fact, our own worst enemy?

Well, I can safely say I have been my own worst enemy for years. It's ruining my personal life. I get that it's my thoughts and feelings that are causing me to suffer. And I understand that people recover from addiction. But knowing that doesn't make my pain go away. I still feel like a failure when it comes to relationships and my sense of self-worth. For me, I have used sex and relationships as a fix. I use people and partners to get high and to find comfort.

And I'm probably addicted to 'drama' too. I mean, how the hell do I 'recover' from that? Don't we all need to feel connected to other human beings?

Christopher: Connected, yes. Addicted, no! We all require a realisation of belongingness and fellowship. And we are all interdependent to a certain extent. The problem lies when we neglect our own mental, emotional and spiritual development. When we are too dependent on any human being (unless we are a baby, a very young child, or ill), then the relationship becomes dysfunctional. And so, if we rely too much on a person for our emotional needs, they will feel either overwhelmed and/or dominate us.

Dr Barbara: The danger here is that when we realise how much we punish ourselves from within, we then go into a spiral of more self-critical thinking, such as: "Goodness, what's wrong with me that I don't know how to manage my thoughts and my feelings? I'm such a failure", which is more of the same.

So we're trapped! How do we get out of that?

Christopher: Thankfully, we don't have to be trapped. The Eastern wisdom traditions describe being trapped in the mind as 'maya', meaning illusion. Maya suggests that we are swept away by our thoughts, emotions, sensations and addictive patterns of behaviour without any awareness.

I've heard of the wisdom traditions. Aren't they ancient scriptures that teach meditation and yoga?

Dr Barbara: Many ancient wisdom traditions offered the kind of guidance that allows us to master our self-awareness for the greater good – a roadmap for life. These days, in mainstream society, we are not given much by way of guidance.

So I have more self-awareness about my addiction, but what next? What can I do right now to stop acting out through my addictions?

Christopher: A common characteristic of untreated addiction is constantly to seek the 'next thing', 'next high' or 'the next fix', and so now is a good time to start being patient. This can be the first new habit that helps to counteract addiction.

Patience? I don't do patience! I want things last week!

Christopher: We can continue to be impatient, but the price we pay is more suffering, dissatisfaction and a lack of serenity. For now, let's just see what it feels like to entertain the possibility of cultivating patience. Give it a go?

Okay then. But can you share anything in your personal experiences about toxic shame and guilt? So far, I feel like it has been mostly me opening up. I feel much more at ease when I can identify with your personal stories.

Dr Barbara: When I was little, I was told I mustn't boast. That to say something good about myself was bad and boastful. So when I got really high marks in tests at school, came top of the class and felt proud and happy about that, I didn't know what to do with those feelings. It felt like it wasn't okay to share them with my parents because they would tell me off for bragging. So being good at something became associated with feeling conflicted and guilty. At the same time, my father put a lot of pressure on me to do well at school and created a very high level of expectation for my future. The emotional messages I received were so confusing. I didn't know what was correct any more. I formed a deep-seated belief that I wasn't okay. That who I was as a person was flawed and wrong. Because that's how it felt when I felt happy that I came first. On the one hand, there was relief that I'd fulfilled my father's expectations. On the other hand, I feel guilty for being cleverer than others and ashamed of the feelings of self-worth this brought me.

Thank you for that, Dr Barbara. It helps to realise that you went through stuff too.

Dr Barbara: We all did. These kinds of turmoil permeate the fabric of our childhoods and generate endless cycles of self-destructive thought patterns, behaviours and feelings. These then become our reality. How about you, Christopher?

Yeah. I would like to hear from you too, Christopher.

Christopher: Before I started to write, I worked in a fiercely competitive industry: the electronic dance music industry. It was very exciting, but aggressive and ruthlessly cut-throat. The obsession to raise your profile in order to connect with the 'right people' was exhausting. Add to this the lethal combination of cocaine, crack, heroin and alcohol that many in the industry are using to just 'keep going' and you will start to get the picture...

Then what happened?

Christopher: Being written off in school as 'below average' fuelled my determination to succeed, which then became a pathological drive. I was terrified of being rejected, of 'not being lovable', which produced an obsession to succeed in the DJ industry. Although I did get many early breaks in my late teens, I felt like a fraud and I resented life.

What happened next?

Christopher: As mentioned earlier, I became heavily addicted to alcohol and cocaine to mask my feelings of being 'unworthy' and 'flawed', even though I was years ahead of the game in the DJ industry. I started to believe I was more human or less human depending on my competitors' profiles and stature. There is a saying in the recovery community that many addicts have a huge ego and zero self-worth. That's quite a complicated mental state to be in.

I can imagine that the bright lights in the DJ world could easily prop up your ego.

Christopher: You're right. You have to be emotionally grounded to work in that industry without self-destructing and I wasn't emotionally prepared in my teens. And so when I talk about addictive cycles, it comes from personal experience. Thankfully, I have been able to address my addictions and have reversed many bad habits. I no longer feel that I don't belong among my fellow human beings.

So both you and Dr Barbara share from personal experience, not just textbook stuff you've read?

Christopher: Yes. I have an addictive personality and I still regularly attend support groups and ask for help. I can't do this alone. Dr Barbara and I both share from personal experience. We, like you, have suffered a great deal.

Dr Barbara: If I hadn't, I don't feel I would have the right to say all the things we're saying here. My academic qualifications are one thing. But my true qualifications are, to my mind, my own rite of passage and what I learnt about myself through my own healing journey. That's why they talk about 'the wounded healer'. And the best I can do is offer what I have learnt with humility and gentleness.

I'm starting to understand this a little bit more. So, my suffering ties in with addiction?

Dr Barbara: We lose touch with an innate sense of ourselves and our own wholeness, with our ability to trust ourselves and know what we are feeling. We forget how to process and relate to our feelings. The human brain is largely an instrument of social interaction. We have all the necessary equipment and abilities that are ready to be primed from birth. For a lot of us, these innate abilities come into conflict with familial, societal and cultural pressures.

We learn to lie, cover up, deny our true sense of a situation, and ignore our gut feelings about people and situations, in order to survive. We get disconnected from our true sense of who we are. People who are the source of security and love have expectations of us; they want us to be a certain way, behave a certain way, and fulfil their own unfulfilled needs.

Can you trace such behaviour growing up?

Dr Barbara: In my family, I was the one who took care of everyone, whether it was making the tea, smoothing the arguments or getting the best grades in school (to take care of my father's need for achievement). I adopted this role to survive within a flawed family system. As a result, I didn't know how to take care of my own needs, how to say what was true for me. I became a carer and a people-pleaser. It comes as no surprise that I married an alcoholic with complete disregard for my own wellbeing. In order to stay safe and get the love that we need as children, we have to play out roles, do things that aren't in our own best interests, and deceive ourselves. So, when later in life, events, people and circumstances trigger the deep-seated chaos in us, we don't know where to turn. Then we find channels of refuge, places to go, things to do, to release the tension, escape from inner conflict and get a sense of being okay, albeit a transient feeling. Places of 'false refuge'.

Christopher: When we seek to escape from inner conflict and pain, we are running away from unresolved childhood trauma or original pain. Most people with serious addictive natures who are in the process of recovery have found that trauma played a huge role in escalating their addictions. It certainly did for me.

That word 'trauma' has such powerful resonance. I thought trauma or PTSD was just for really serious issues like the stress that comes from war or a terrible accident?

Christopher: Trauma affects most of us. Unfortunately, a person with an addictive nature reacts to trauma in a destructive way. I don't think I've ever met an addict in long-term recovery who hasn't gone through at least one traumatic childhood experience. Research indicates that one traumatic event in childhood is as grave as continuous combat in a war zone. A traumatic event during childhood can leave a grave imprint on the human body. Thankfully, however, this can be reversed.

Dr Barbara: Absolutely. Maybe not reversed, but overwritten so that it doesn't exert the same dire control over our behaviour. That's the beauty of what we now know through modern neuroscience. Until about twenty years ago, and certainly when I was at medical school in the 1970s, we were taught that the brain was fixed, that nerve cells died progressively over time and that was that. Now we know that the opposite is true. The way your brain is today is the result of the way you've used it and lived your life to date. The brain is a living tissue that adapts and changes to the experiences we have. No one comes out of the womb with the word 'addict' stamped on their bottom.

Fascinating. I want to know more about how addiction relates to my brain.

Dr Barbara: The brain is changing and responding moment by moment. New inputs create new neural connections and pathways – new learning – all the time. Most of the time, we have been unaware about the 'programming' that has shaped our brains. When we were younger, we had little choice about how our lives were lived and the way people treated us. Our brains and the beliefs we have about ourselves got shaped accordingly, without our conscious intervention. Now, there's a rather fancy expression that's currently being used a lot: self-directed neuroplasticity.

Neuro what? That sounds fancy!

Dr Barbara: Yes! It's not really that fancy when you unravel it. What it means is that by intentionally directing our thinking, feelings, actions and awareness, we are actually creating the possibility of altering the way our brains work. Thoughts alone can alter the substrate of the brain. When we engage in mental activity, this is represented by electrochemical reactions in the brain. One neuron fires off and connects with another according to the habitual pathway already laid down. We mentioned this earlier.

Yes, I remember that. I got the image of one of those old fashioned switchboard at a telephone exchange. I used to see them in movies. All those wires and plugs being moved around.

Dr Barbara: I like that! That's a good image. Every time you think a thought you have had many times before, you are reinforcing an existing neural pathway, making it stronger – connecting the jacks at the telephone exchange into the same old sockets, if you like. More often than not, the thoughts we have about ourselves are self-critical, judgemental and geared towards blame, guilt and shame. It's as if those operators at the telephone exchange can't remove the jacks from their sockets. Every time you make a choice to express gratitude, kindness towards yourself, generosity or just notice what is going on in your life in a new way, you are creating neural connections and pathways that hardwire these behaviours. Thus, to use your image, new telephone wires and their jacks are being plugged into new sockets on the switchboard or into existing sockets but in a new way.

I can see that.

Dr Barbara: The more you repeat these new patterns, the quicker they wire into the brain. Repetition is an important part of learning. Whenever you learn something new, the brain changes activity and eventually changes shape. For example, if you practise mindfulness for six weeks every day, at the end of that practice, the patterns of activity in your brain will look different in an MRI scanner from how they did six weeks earlier. We have the power to transform our experience of ourselves in this moment. As we repeatedly do this, we are wiring our neural pathways towards greater self-awareness. Like any skill that we practise, as we do so, it gets easier. It's an upward spiral that will shift us out of the depths of our suffering. This is what happened to me.

I'm really interested in this. There was an awful lot of dysfunction, fighting and unbearable tension in my childhood. I can't remember that far back though. Do you think I was affected by trauma?

Christopher: I can't speak for you, but if you do feel you were affected by childhood trauma and need to grieve original pain, it is possible to transcend self-detrimental habits and damaging perceptions. However, it's essential to remember that recovery is a very slow process. There are no shortcuts. It's important to be aware that many families are dysfunctional, but we can change the patterns. Even if a child grew up in an aggressive or addictive household, they can heal and move past that with immense emotional resilience, wisdom and gratitude. This is what recovery can offer anyone who, like you, is open-minded, willing and ready to explore self-awareness and take action.

I hope so.

Dr Barbara: I think it's really important to say again that this is, in some way, part of the human condition. Everyone goes through cycles of learning, being stuck, pain, growth and release. Most people desire refuge and solace outside of themselves. In sex, drugs, food, even shopping! Few of us have been taught how to find refuge within ourselves. This is a big black hole in education in our society that is leading to much pain and unhappiness. Stress, anxiety and depression are predicted to be the biggest causes of ill health in our society by 2020. That's just a few years away. And it's mostly because we haven't been shown how to access the huge treasure trove of inner resources that we all have inside ourselves, abilities we have always had – resources we hope we are showing you how to develop.

That's a harrowing prediction. I also suffer from anxiety and stress. I find that it compounds my addictions. Whenever I get stressed or anxious at work or start worrying about finances, I start seeking ways to fix myself.

Christopher: I can identify with that. The fear of economic hardship emotionally triggers most people. Addicts who are not in recovery will often 'act out' whenever they feel stressed, strained, anxious or afraid. The gambling addict might gamble when feeling anxious. The codependent will try to control people when they feel stressed and powerless because of a vicissitude. The drug addict will use a substance, the alcoholic will try to 'fix himself' with alcohol, and the sex and love addict will act out accordingly when circumstances appear to be challenging or overwhelming.

I can relate to all of those patterns. I don't necessarily use the same fixes as the examples you have given, but I literally have to fill my discontentment with fixes. The problem is my 'highs' never bring me happiness. They always make me feel worthless and disgusting after the crash. I hate it! So those highs I seek when I feel like acting out must do something to my brain? I literally feel my mind is altering when the addict mindset kicks in.

Dr Barbara: That 'high' feeling is when the brain releases a pleasure hormone called dopamine, which makes us feel good. Addiction has hijacked the healthy causes of feeling good, so we get bursts of dopamine in relation to our addictive behaviour. Then we crave that 'feel-good' feeling. Except, of course, it doesn't really feel good, not deep down. In addiction, it takes less and less to trigger our craving (what is called 'sensitivity') and more and more to satisfy it (what is known as 'tolerance').

I actually feel temporarily 'high' in the lead-up to acting out. It's like leading up to oblivion. Does this make sense?

Dr Barbara: Actually, the biggest release of dopamine comes in the anticipation phase, in the build-up and chase for whatever the source of our addiction is. The actual act of indulging is always followed by a precipitous drop in dopamine and we feel lousy again. But lousy is how we're used to feeling, if we're honest with ourselves. So we don't associate the lousiness as being caused by the addiction. We just see the addiction as a way to escape the feeling lousy. Once we start to recognise this deep-seated feeling of discomfort as the backdrop to our experience of ourselves, it allows us to start disentangling addictive behaviour.

I never used to be like this. I used to be a quiet and playful child who just wanted everyone and me to be happy. Then, gradually, I started to feel more and more mentally isolated and angry towards myself and my life. My childhood memories are very blurry, but it's as if my feelings are trying to tell me something. That's how I could identify with the cocaine addict I met in the bar, even though our patterns and fixes are different.

Christopher: That's a massive realisation!

I've learnt to master good habits in my professional life but I've always neglected to create healthy habits in my personal and romantic life. I guess that is one of my blind spots.

Christopher: We all have blind spots, but if we are open-minded and reach out to others for help, we can change our behaviour a lot quicker. It's much easier to change our behaviour if we have the right kind of support.

I get that. It makes sense. I have mentors who assist me in my professional life but I've never thought about using that same method in my personal relationships. I'm really starting to see the power of self-denial in my own life. So you think it's possible to learn new 'tricks'? I thought you couldn't teach an old dog new tricks?

Dr Barbara: The brain changes shape according to how we use it. As we speak together and it seems you are having insights and realisations, new neural connections are firing up. We can learn skills and acquire tools, ways of being that allow us to intentionally alter the way our brains are wired for the better. As we examined before, we now know that, through our own consciousness and intention, we can create new neural pathways. Mind is creating matter. In fact, we're doing it all the time. Even in the course of this conversation, when little 'light-bulb' moments arise, we are actively altering the substrate of our brain. We can learn skills, acquire tools and understand ways of being that facilitate these changes so that it is easier for us to release ourselves from destructive patterns.

That's exciting! So I'm not stuck for life – thank goodness for that!

Christopher: We are very lucky to be alive in the twenty-first century. We have more understanding with respect to addiction, original pain work, trauma and mindfulness than in any other time in human history. People who were suffering from addiction, even as recently as seventy years ago, were ostracised from society and had no effective emotional treatment or help. They overdosed (if they were hooked on a substance), died a lonely death, or were doomed to settle for a miserable existence.

That is something to be grateful for. So what now?

Dr Barbara: The first step is to start looking within ourselves and facing the truth. At some point in our lives, things happen that encourage us to look deep within. Things happen that precipitate an existential crisis. A broken marriage, a death in the family, being fired, waking up in the middle of a field with no idea how you got there, a gaping hole in your bank statement, an irregular heartbeat, or hospital admission. At this point, it's like life is falling apart.

I can definitely relate to that!

Dr Barbara: This huge hole, tear or rip has appeared in the fabric of our everyday reality. Actually, this disaster is the opening we require. We can peer through that hole, through the illusion and fabric of lies that have become our reality and see something new. It may be just a glimpse before the hole seals up again. But that glimpse will be enough to feed another part of our being. The part that longs to heal. Longs to be whole. Longs to be free from the pain we are drowning out with the noise of our addiction. Deep inside, we long to give up the false refuge that is destroying us. And this moment of crisis – that tear in the fabric of our tightly stitched reality – can be the opportunity that this part deep inside us needs. Have you heard that lovely saying about cracks being where the light gets in?

To me, this sounds like hitting rock bottom. I often feel I am close to that place, if I'm honest.

Christopher: You're very fortunate.

I beg your pardon? I'm fortunate for hitting rock bottom? Are you mad?

Christopher: You're lucky because, as a result of hitting rock bottom, you will be more willing to look inside yourself. I've met hundreds of addicts who are still in denial about their behaviour. So, in that sense, you are very fortunate. It means you can start to heal.

I haven't thought about it like that. I suppose the saying is true: 'the darkest hour is just before the dawn'. So would my rock bottom be similar to the cocaine addict I met in the bar or an anorexic who checks into rehab?

Christopher: Hitting bottom is an inside job – it's something that happens within our consciousness. We might, as Dr Barbara said, have to go through a nasty divorce, go bankrupt or even just wake up one morning full of despair, but the pain is inside of us. External events can provoke us to get to a place where we feel compelled to reach out and ask for help.

How do you stop that chink of light from closing up again? How do you stay in touch with that sense of what is possible?

Christopher: By connecting with people who have had similar experiences and have rebuilt wholesome lives. There are plenty of people who can assist you who have come through the worst of addiction and trauma. For example, if a drug addict continues to associate with other drug addicts who are still using drugs, they stand little chance of recovering. If, however, they seek to associate with people who are in recovery, their chances of addressing addiction look promising. You know the saying, 'birds of a feather flock together' and so on.

That makes sense. My cousin almost died of anorexia and after she checked out of rehab, she said she had to stop associating with women who were not in recovery. Otherwise, she could find herself being drawn back into old patterns like competing to see who could starve themselves the most. She's much better now.

Dr Barbara: Seek support. Find people who will not judge you. Who deeply appreciate what you're going through. Who know how slippery the mind can be and have the skills to nurture your desire to heal. Without making you feel wrong. Without pulling their own power trip on you. People who have compassion, wisdom and humility. Most of all, know that suffering is part of the human condition. The task ahead is one we all have, if we are honest with ourselves. You are not alone.

That makes a lot of sense. I do tend to attract addicts who are not in recovery, and I have sought refuge from people who are very judgemental and bordering on abusive.

Christopher: The people we associate with and the environments in which we spend time have a tremendous impact on our mental, emotional, spiritual, social and financial wellbeing. That's always a good thing to remember.

You're saying all this as if it were easy. But these habits and patterns run deep. Doesn't that mean years of therapy to get to the bottom of all that mess inside our heads? Well, in my head anyway?

Dr Barbara: Understanding why you are the way you are is great – really important. It helps you get a handle on things. But it won't necessarily shift things beyond the level of the intellect. It might not release emotional energy and break down the patterns and neural pathways wired into the brain.

Oh, so what else then?

Dr Barbara: What we're aiming to convey in this book is a way to find a transformed relationship with yourself, a place of compassion and acceptance. A place where you can experience yourself as whole and complete. You're not broken. Bits of your behaviour are self-destructive, but who you are, your true spirit, is always there. That's the bit that woke up when the light came through the hole in the fabric, which we talked about earlier. So the questions become: "How can I water the seed of this sense of myself? How can I allow that part of me that I glimpsed through the crack to flourish and grow?" This is another step forward from realising how you got where you are.

Thanks. They are very helpful questions.

Christopher: Just as Dr Barbara said, intellect might be helpful but it alone isn't sufficient to bring about change. The process of recovering from addictiveness happens at a deeper level of consciousness and through feeling our pain without using any old addictive fixes. There is no escaping that getting in touch with our original pain is the touchstone to mental, emotional and spiritual wellbeing. Grieving our original pain (dysfunction in our family of origin) is different from the suffering caused by acting out in addictive behaviour. Processing our original pain leads to contentment, happiness and authentic success. As the Zen Master, Thich Nhat Hanh, said, "You cannot grow lotus flowers on marble. You have to grow them in mud."

As much as I hate feeling pain, I'm ready to continue. Nothing can be worse than being isolated in my addictive suffering. I feel ready to listen some more.

Dr Barbara: Pain is another one of these words, like suffering, that has strong connotations. Take a step back right now and release any feeling of pressure and anxiety that the word might evoke in you. It's safe. It's okay. Right now, you are okay. There are no scary monsters under the bed! Rest in the awareness that, right now, you are okay. Breathe! Feel your breath. Get in touch with that. Get in touch with what is true for you in this moment. As we learn to allow ourselves to drop down into the present moment, we see that fear is also an illusion. As we learn to embrace fear, we are no longer afraid of it. Now there's a conundrum for you!

CHAPTER FOUR

Mind the Gap?

Dr Barbara: As Christopher has said, one of the main things to change in our understanding of addiction is this feeling of isolation. That we are alone, that no one else is as broken as we are, and that we must, at all costs, hide this sense of ourselves and run from it.

But that's how it has felt most of my life, as far as I can remember. And I've always had a difficult time trusting my senses and gut reactions.

Dr Barbara: And maybe it might help to hear that you are not alone in that feeling of being alone! I know that's how I used to feel. In many of the wisdom traditions, particularly Buddhism, it is clearly expressed that suffering (that word again) is part of being human.

I don't like the word 'suffering'.

Dr Barbara: What I understand from it is that there is no one in the world who isn't fighting some kind of battle on the inside. Realising that helped me accept my own suffering. Something inside me said, "Oh, okay. So there is no bed of roses. In that case, maybe I'd better find a different way to relate to the difficulties life seems to keep throwing at me, a way in that I don't take it all so personally."

Ah, I see. So understanding that, just by being human, there will be stuff that goes 'wrong', it's not your fault and you have a better way to relate to the challenges rather than using them as evidence that you're a bad person?

Dr Barbara: Yes, exactly. So the quest becomes not "How can I get rid of my suffering?" but "How can I meet it with equanimity and balance?", "How can I rearrange my internal landscape to include upset, difficulties and inadequacies as a part of life, rather than as signs that I am broken?" and "How can I come to a place where I have other ways to ease my pain than indulging in self-destructive patterns and habits? How can I find that place of refuge inside myself?"

Because that is possible. I really hope this message is coming through: you are not alone. And yes, it is possible.

Yes. I am starting to feel less isolated.

Christopher: Accepting suffering is a massive breakthrough. If we can accept that we will feel pain on the journey, we won't take it too personally. When responding to life with equanimity, we can lessen the impact of mental and emotional suffering.

So do you still suffer? Do you still feel pain, Christopher?

Christopher: Of course. I am afraid of many things, but I have developed the habit of facing my fears, one day at a time. I feel emotional pain and anger but it passes much more quickly now that I have the ability to be mindful and present. I still grieve and cry when it is necessary to do so. Just as Dr Barbara said, suffering is part of the human condition, but we can learn to transcend it and live peacefully even when it all hits the fan.

What about you, Dr Barbara? Do you still suffer?

Dr Barbara: Yes. Only my relationship to it has shifted. Rather than feeling subsumed by my feelings, it's as if they occur in a space. They don't drown me. I'm aware of them. I notice my tendency to first judge and then resist. A major shift for me occurred in being able to identify these passing sensations and thoughts as just that: passing sensations and thoughts. It's as if I am the vessel in which they are contained, rather than they filling up every molecule of my reality right to the brim. Sometimes, it can take a while for me to come to this place inside myself. But I have tools that help me. Like cultivating an intention to be kind to myself and to accept rather than resist what already is. It's a practice, an ongoing journey of self-discovery and growth.

It never occurred to me that everyone is suffering. I tend to look at other people and idealise them. It looks like their lives are okay, that they've got it all together. But I guess they're doing the same as me, presenting a kind of "Look how okay I am" mask to the world.

Dr Barbara: Oh boy, I know that one! Until you get to the point where the cost of pretending is greater than the cost of being vulnerable and saying it like it is. Like the cocaine addict in the bar that night.

I do hope I can pluck up enough courage to continue revealing my fears.

Christopher: To constantly pretend that we are okay when we are not is incredibly tiring. By sharing our feelings with non-shaming friends and being in touch with our hearts, we start to feel liberated and free. Today, I continue to be honest with friends about my emotional state, knowing that my awareness of today's feelings actually transcends the emotions. If I am feeling pain, it's better to own it. And if I'm feeling upbeat, it's better to share this too. Joyful moments, angry moments – they are all part of one continuous cycle.

I would love to be liberated but my thoughts are just so draining. My mind can be like a war zone at times. I could do with a lot more mindfulness.

Dr Barbara: The thing is, most of us are lost in our thoughts a lot of the time. We live in our heads with a kind of chatter going on, a constant narrative, about who we are, how we are, what we've done, should or shouldn't have done, ought to do, ought not to do, what we'll have for dinner, why that person looked at us that way, and so on – an endless stream of thoughts, basically.

Yup, I can go along with that.

Dr Barbara: Most of the time, most of us think that we are our thoughts. We identify with our thoughts as if they were real. They're not. We are not our thoughts. We have thoughts. A major breakthrough comes when you get to see these thoughts for what they are: just thoughts. Electrochemical activity in the brain – the same thoughts going round and round. Around forty thousand to fifty thousand of them a day, and ninety-nine per cent the same or versions of the same theme.

That's insane! I never thought about that…

Dr Barbara: We don't give ourselves the chance to sit back and notice the flow of thoughts. How about trying this? Stop right now. Look at the phone you're holding. Look at your hand holding it. Just that. Notice the colour of your skin. Feel the point of contact between your skin and what you are holding. Stay with that for a moment. Get inside the experience of that feeling of your skin touching the phone. In this simple moment of stillness, you may hear your thoughts. Let your thoughts be. Let them pass. Return to an awareness right now of your hand. Can you hear the chatter in your head?

Yes, I can hear the mental chatter because you've reminded me that I have it. I find it really hard to let my thoughts be, especially when I'm thinking negatively. It's like I get stuck in a train of thought and it spirals out of control.

Christopher: Generally speaking, it's our thoughts that create fear and upsetting stories in our minds. Thoughts are like images that appear on the screen of our minds. They are like TV adverts that repeat themselves over and over. Those images (thoughts) gradually intertwine into a self-made mental story about our lives – similar to creating a storyline for a film. Unfortunately, our thoughts make us suffer when we continue to completely identify with them.

I identify with that. My thoughts seem to be very real and they never shut up. Some days, they are so draining.

Dr Barbara: We buy into our own story. Bringing ourselves back to the present sometimes feels like dragging ourselves away from a bad but compelling movie. You just noticed your thought rather than being eaten up by it. Ask yourself now: who had those thoughts?

Well, me I guess.

Dr Barbara: Exactly. So a little gap opened up between you and your thoughts. That's great!

Oh … I get it! I saw my thought as a thought. How cool!

Dr Barbara: The thing is that most of our thoughts are not very complimentary to ourselves. We have deep-seated beliefs and attitudes that find expression in a constant stream of thoughts, what I call the chattering monkeys. Beliefs that were wired into our brains when we were little. One of mine is, "Nothing I do will ever be good enough." Another one is, "If I am really me, people will laugh, I'll look stupid." Another is: "It's all my fault." Whenever anything goes wrong, I have this knee-jerk reaction that it's somehow my fault. Which means it's my job to fix it. Maybe that's why I became a doctor! As kids, when we see our parents or the people around us unhappy, we feel as if it's our fault. It's not a logical thing. As small children, we don't have that capacity to think it through. We just soak up the vibe and feel bad. That feeling then becomes the water we swim in, which can be really hard to see.

Christopher: Mental stories can literally spoil a human life. It took me a long time to become aware of my mental commentary, such as: "Everything always goes wrong", "I won't be accepted", "I'm a failure" or "What's the point?" Those fears were deep-rooted and triggered many upsetting addictive patterns of behaviour.

In my family, my parents often argued and then I'd hide in the cupboard. When I came out, I'd get into trouble for being in the cupboard. Which was really confusing, because the cupboard was my safe place. I would feel guilty and ashamed. But looking at it now, I can see I was just trying to protect myself.

Dr Barbara: Yes, I really get that. We all find ways to create safe places for ourselves. We have to, to soothe ourselves. To find comfort from the hurt and confusion. This is natural. It all gets a bit more twisted when doing what it takes to keep ourselves safe also becomes wrong in the eyes of the people from whom we seek love and stability. Then there's no way out.

Christopher: Yes, those mixed messages at an early age can be terribly confusing. Sadly, painful childhood events leave an imprint on the human body and a murky residue in adulthood.

So I'm doomed?

Dr Barbara: I don't think that's what Christopher is saying here. The great thing is that, as adults, we can start to unpick some of these tangles. As we learn to observe our thoughts, rather than believe them, we can discern the deep-seated beliefs that run us. There is enormous freedom in this. More importantly, perhaps, we can start to get in touch with how we feel.

I'm not sure I want to do that!

Dr Barbara: Ha ha! I know what you mean! In our culture, being in touch with our feelings is not something we're very good at! There's a huge disconnect for a lot of us. The thing is that a thought in itself is, as we said, just electrochemical activity in the brain. We can teach robots to think like humans. The thought "The bus is late and I'm going to be late for work" is just a thought. What gives it 'charge' is the feeling that accompanies it and what we make of it.

Yeah. I get that.

Dr Barbara: Maybe your heart beats a little faster, your tummy churns and your forehead gets knotted. You feel anxious. Then you start to think about what your boss will say, and this further fuels your feeling of anxiousness. This is what Eckhart Tolle talks about as mental-emotional reaction patterns. What is fascinating to me as a scientist is that we can now understand how this automatic reaction is wired into the brain. And what is so exciting is that we now know the brain changes shape according to how you use it.

That's very interesting.

Dr Barbara: The main skill we need to learn is that of mindful self-awareness, the ability to be present to our thoughts and feelings rather than drown in them. To allow and accept them, not fight them, and understand that we are not these thoughts and feelings. We are the space in which they occur.

You mean by being mindful of my thoughts and feelings, my life will improve and my addictive behaviour will slow down?

Christopher: Yes. When we are mindful of our thoughts and feelings, they cannot control our behaviour and we can detach from them. For instance, there is a classic saying in the addiction recovery community: "Take the needle off the record."

What do you mean by that? Are you referring to vinyl?

Christopher: Well, I used to play records for a living in nightclubs (back then, DJs used vinyl rather than laptops). Whenever a record would get stuck in a groove (meaning it would jump), I would pick the needle off the record and, consequently, there would be silence.

I remember records.

Christopher: Well, just like taking the needle off the record, you can pause and pay attention to the senses – the external sounds you hear and the flow of the breath. This will silence the mind because you will not be the mind. You have transcended it.

Wow. That makes sense to me. I just had a light-bulb moment.

Christopher: That's great.

I did have a light-bulb moment, but now my thoughts have just flooded my mind again. Being mindful is so hard to do. I've heard meditation can help, but I've never really tried to do it properly. It's just quite alien to me and I would feel odd sitting in the lotus position.

Christopher: Look how quickly your mind started to race after a few seconds of stillness. Notice how self-doubt started to take you away from your mindful, sense-awareness practice.

Yeah, I felt self-doubt. It's a horrible feeling.

Christopher: The fear and loud thoughts were just that: emotions and sensations. It's important to point out we cannot fight our thoughts or force our mind to be still. We can only observe the breath and mind activity.

How will observing my breathing help to shut my mind up?

Dr Barbara: You can't shut your mind up. That's not what we are aiming to do. We can, however, let it be, notice what it's saying and get that, in this moment, just noticing the flow of thought fundamentally alters our relationship to that flow.

Christopher: When we observe the flow of our breathing, we transcend our thoughts and are able to bring mind and body into harmony with each other. Thus, we create calm.

Yes, but my thoughts won't stop.

Christopher: Your thoughts will always be there, chattering away. It's the identification with them that alters. We learn to allow the thoughts and to let them be. To let them pass. To neither resist, want to alter or give in to them.

What about when I feel like fixing my addictive behaviour? How will breathing help? Surely it can't be that easy?

Christopher: No one said healing from addiction or learning to be mindful was going to be easy. Simple, yes. Easy, no! When you develop the habit of anchoring yourself to the present through your breath, the momentum of addiction starts to dissolve. The nowness of life sweeps away addictive mental commentary and static emotional energy.

Dr Barbara: Thoughts and beliefs are like boxes that we've been living inside of all these years with the lid firmly shut. Once we see a belief system for what it is, it doesn't have the same hold over us any more. My "Nothing I do will ever be enough" belief doesn't run me any more. I notice when it pops up and see it as a habit.

That must be very liberating.

Dr Barbara: It is. As I've practised meditation over the years, it's as if the glue that holds the lid on the boxes has dissolved. And the other side of it is that, as we slow things down and sit in stillness, we start to access a place where we feel whole, complete and at peace. Like the stillness beneath the choppy waves of the sea.

Like when you dive under water in the swimming pool and it's all quiet.

Dr Barbara: Yes. That's a place inside us that is always there and always will be, that cannot be destroyed or taken away from us no matter what we go through in life. Hold on to that. Rest assured that who you are is whole and complete.

That's a comforting idea.

Dr Barbara: Part of the transformation of our relationships to our addictive behaviours is realising this space within ourselves. It might feel like there's a huge gap between where you are now and an experience of this space. Actually, there isn't. It takes no time at all to find that space because it's always there.

So if I practise finding that place inside me, it will be easier to find it when things get tricky?

Dr Barbara: Yes. And through self-compassion, acceptance and forgiveness, we can include the wounded part of ourselves, the bits we don't like or even hate. We can integrate the aspects that we feel we need to expurgate. And by so doing, through this acceptance, we heal. We accept and integrate rather than try to expunge or wipe away. This impulse to get rid of or wipe away actually brings more resistance and pain.

Acceptance, compassion, forgiveness. Those are big words. They all sound a bit religious, if you don't mind me saying so.

Dr Barbara: Not at all. I get it. In our society, anything that has to do with the goodness of being human does tend to be given those kind of connotations. I prefer the word 'spiritual'. Religions tend to be about systems of belief. That's not what we're talking about here.

I'm glad to hear that.

Dr Barbara: I'm aware that the word 'spiritual' can cause some eyebrows to be raised. Actually, I'd like to reinstate the word. For me, it means doing what it takes to move ourselves along a spectrum. Personally, I want to move myself along that spectrum, towards being my best person. I have a long way to go, but the intention is there. I try to embrace certain core tenets as pillars around which to base my actions, attitudes and intentions. These include generosity, self-awareness, personal responsibility, forgiveness and compassion. If that makes me spiritual, then bring it on!

I respect that. I can get my head around your perspective on spirituality. And what you seem to be saying is that having this intention is what moves us forward in relation to our addictions.

Dr Barbara: Yes! Hold on to that! And honour the impulse to uncover your innate goodness. Are you ready to move on?

Yes.

CHAPTER FIVE

Me, Myself and I

You've talked about feelings a lot, and that leaves me feeling a little on edge. I have always pushed my emotions down because when I do feel them, it becomes intense and sometimes, I panic.

Dr Barbara: Nicely observed! An important step towards making friends with our feelings is being aware of how we are feeling right now.

Making friends with our feelings? What do you mean? How do we do that?

Dr Barbara: While thoughts can drive us insane, it's the ability to be emotionally literate that drives us sane. Emotions are what make us human, bring us together and can drive us apart. Decision-making is largely emotion-driven, not intellect-based. Think of all the major decisions you have made in your life. You probably weighed the pros and cons in your mind. And then you went with your gut. Our ability to be in touch with ourselves depends on our ability to be aware of our feelings. And feelings are grounded in the body.

Yeah. My body feels really tense when I'm angry and feels very warm and fuzzy when I feel happy.

Christopher: Our feelings are powerful. Without training on how to be emotionally intelligent, feelings can be extremely difficult to live with. To make peace with our feelings is to acknowledge how we are feeling in this moment rather than trying to suppress them. And, as you have identified, we can process our feelings a lot more easily when we are in tune with the body.

Dr Barbara: And the good news is that we already have all the hardware in our brains to be innately emotionally intelligent. It's as if some software got uploaded that gets in the way. So all we are doing is reigniting skills and abilities we already have.

Yes, but how does this relate to my addictions?

Dr Barbara: Let's think about what drives us to carry on doing things that damage us. At some level, we feel bad and maybe we don't realise it. But experience has shown us that if we indulge in our habit, we will get a sense of relief. So we indulge in our false friend, our 'false refuge'. And then ... we're back to square one, with feelings of worthlessness, self-hate, anger, sadness and fear. That then drives us round the vicious circle again to seek relief.

But I don't like feeling angry, sad or anxious. I don't want to be in touch with that.

Dr Barbara: Yes, and feelings are like thoughts. They come and go like the weather. What would it be like to be in touch with your emotions, to be okay with them, knowing that, like the weather, they too will pass?

To be able to say, "Right now I'm feeling tense"? And just notice that?

Dr Barbara: Yes. This is an important aspect of self-awareness, to know our emotional state. In our society, we tend to judge feelings as good or bad. We want to avoid the ones we judge as 'bad' and strive for the ones we consider to be 'good'.

What are you saying then? That we just accept feelings as feelings without judgement?

Dr Barbara: It's an intriguing idea, isn't it? Most people are chasing happiness as if it were a thing out there to grab. They then push away or deny what they are actually feeling, as if it were bad. Maybe it's this constant see-saw of avoidance and grasping that keeps us stuck.

What's the alternative? Is there one?

Dr Barbara: What would it be like if we were able to sit with our sadness, anger or fear and welcome it as a friend? Knowing it is a temporary state that will pass, if we can allow it to?

When we can be aware of our emotions, in touch with what we are feeling, we can accept that this is what is happening right now. It's already happening, so resisting it is like saying you don't have a nose.

Or like going out in the rain and saying it's not raining? Or complaining about it?

Dr Barbara: Good point. When we accept what is, we transform our relationship to it. We enter that place where we are whole and complete, and find peace, power and the potential to create new possibilities. This is not an intellectual process. This is experiential. It's quite hard to capture what this is in words. But I hope you're getting a sense of it.

Yes, I can see that by being okay about how I am feeling and noticing rather than resisting or suppressing it, I can have a healthier relationship with my emotions and that, then, I might get a handle on my addictive responses. Is this where emotional intelligence comes into play?

Christopher: Yes. If we can delay gratification, demonstrate self-awareness and share our feelings with emotionally intelligent human beings, we can temper addictive urges and save ourselves a lot of distress.

I need to get more in touch with my feelings. I can accept that. But what about when I feel like my mind is caving in? When no matter what I do, I feel completely stuck in a cycle of confusion and restlessness? That is when I usually act out in my addictive behaviour. I mean, what choice do I have?

Christopher: We always have a choice. In other words, we can make conscious choices that, no matter how bad we feel, we will not break our addictive bottom lines.

Bottom lines?

Christopher: Bottom lines are addictive behaviours that we make a conscious choice not to repeat. For example, a recovering cocaine addict would create a bottom line that they will not use a mind- or mood-altering substance to deliberately get high. A recovering sex addict might create a bottom line not to watch pornography or not to have sex without any emotional or spiritual connection. Bottom lines are a symbol of our intentions and are very useful at a practical level to address addictions. In many recovery communities, twelve-step fellowships and addiction rehabs, there is also a concept called 'top lines'.

I get the 'bottom lines' concept. They make sense. But what are top lines?

Christopher: Top lines to a human being who tends to isolate (an avoidant) would mean they make an effort to talk to another human being when the opportunity arises. A top line can also mean that, whether we feel like it or not, we are committed to our recovery and to improving our emotional and professional life. The idea of 'top lines' is not to be hard on ourselves or to put us in a position where we feel unsafe or burnt out. It's a way to avoid missing opportunities to learn, serve and grow.

But what is actually happening to me when I feel hopeless? What about when I call a friend and find myself unable to communicate how I feel?

Dr Barbara: When we experience profound emotion, relive a past trauma, or something happens that knocks us for six, the part of the brain responsible for speech and language shuts down. It literally goes offline. This is why talking about things can be difficult and can have limited value sometimes. But by getting in touch with a feeling, in a safe setting, with an intention for healing and kindness towards ourselves, this presence allows a remoulding of neural pathways.

Aha. So this is why I can't articulate my emotions when I feel raw and static?

Dr Barbara: Yes. This is really important because most addictive behaviours have their roots in unresolved emotional patterns and experiences. Like you in your cupboard, me with my exam results. That unresolvable inner turmoil gets buried in your soma, in your body, in your muscle memory. Later events can trigger this memory in an illogical way. Then we get upset and don't know why. That scares us. So we turn to our false friend, our addictive pattern, for refuge. It's the path of least resistance in the brain. We find refuge there, albeit temporarily. That gives us a sense of reward and drives future repetitions of the avoidance strategy.

So when my unresolvable inner turmoil is triggered in my body, this is why I quickly turn to fixing myself on temporary highs and destructive behaviour?

Christopher: Yes. This is where body scan or body awareness meditation comes into play. Are you aware of body scan meditation?

I think I've heard of it. Isn't it connected to mindfulness?

Christopher: Yes, it is. Body scan meditation is mentally scanning through each part of the body with presence. It helps us be one with the body. Thus, we can feel if we are holding on to any tension or heaviness or any static emotions. And by doing so, we can find relief and internal freedom.

Will this actually help me to keep track of my addictive thinking? I get a little bit sceptical when people mention new-age practices.

Christopher: Body scan meditation has been practised for over two thousand years – there is nothing 'new' about it. And yes, we can temper our addictive thinking by practising it. Our mind begins to clear when we honour how our bodies feel and go deep within.

Sometimes this practice brings a subtle feeling of self-acceptance, and sometimes it can awaken profound realisations of bliss and joy in our consciousness.

That sounds really good for me. I would like to try that.

Dr Barbara: All emotions are physiological patterns of change in our bodies. Like an increase in heart rate, tensing of the jaw muscles, clenching of the fists, or changes in breathing. By becoming more aware of what is happening in our body, moment by moment, we are becoming more aware of subtle changes in how we feel. Emotions or feelings are rooted in our body. To stay in touch with ourselves and our emotions is to be in touch with these changes in the physiological state, right now, as they happen. Staying in touch with the feelings and sensations brings us out of our heads and breaks automatic patterns. In this way, we can learn to recognise our reactive patterns and learn to make different choices in response to them.

Is this where the mind and body connection comes into play?

Dr Barbara: The body, the emotions and the mind are all you, are all deeply connected. Feelings are grounded in the body. The brain interprets physical sensations, and habitual processes create the mental interpretation of these feelings as thoughts. These habitual ways of thinking and interpreting events perpetuate the cycle and further add to the feeling. By being more aware of our bodies, we are more in touch with our emotions. By being more aware of our feelings, we can learn to accept them. By learning to accept, we ease our resistance, which is the source of our pain. We can release habitual patterns by awareness and attention to what is happening now.

I believe you, but is there any scientific or medical evidence to back this up?

Dr Barbara: Basically, we can think of there being three operating systems. One is geared towards achievement, motivation and moving forward and is driven by dopamine. The second is driven by adrenalin, and is activated by fear, being upset, and the need to avoid. The third is where we feel safe, calm, connected and complete. Oxytocin is the main brain chemical at work here. Addiction is fuelled by dopamine.

That makes sense…

Dr Barbara: Stress and emotions that we are avoiding trigger the adrenalin-based system, the fight-or-flight response. Mindfulness and contemplative techniques activate the third system. So does love, kindness, hugging, meaningful conversation and intimacy. To overcome addiction, we want to maximise activity in this third circle, minimise activity in the fight-or-flight circle and redirect motivation towards our deep-seated desire to be driven by the impulse to change. To find freedom within.

That's fascinating.

CHAPTER SIX

All you need is ... love?

Something I've noticed is when I'm feeling good, everything is easy and when I'm feeling physically ill or I've 'acted out' in my addiction, it feels like everything is falling apart. Why can't my feelings be straightforward and less complicated?

Christopher: Many of us feel the same way you do. We all have days when we feel down and days when we feel upbeat. It's important to realise you're not alone.

Dr Barbara: An important step of our growth as human beings is the realisation that what we are experiencing and going through is what human beings have been struggling with for centuries. You are not alone. It's part of the human condition. That might sound a bit heavy but, actually, if you can get your head around this, it lightens the load. There's nothing wrong with us if we go through different and sometimes difficult states of mind. All of us go through these things. The ancient wisdom traditions studied the stages and spaces of the inner landscape and created guidance. They understood deeply what it is to be human, and taught people ways to navigate it. Ways to greet these difficult times with warmth and compassion rather than fear and dread.

One day I feel on top of the world, and the next I feel self-doubt. Sometimes I feel depressed even when everything is going my way, and sometimes I feel good when nothing much is happening in my life. I hate this about myself.

Christopher: We all have the potential to resent ourselves. We can all direct hate inwards and feel unworthy of peace and joy, but it doesn't have to be that way. We can learn to love and take care of ourselves.

Some of the things I say to myself are really cruel. Sometimes, I wish I was someone else.

Christopher: Try not to beat yourself up. You were not born with self-hatred. We learnt self-hatred from our parents or guardians, family of origin and society. Why not consider the notion of developing self-compassion instead? Once we start to untangle what might seem like the complications of our varying mental and emotion patterns, we start to see that there is a way through.

Did you say self-compassion? You mean self-esteem, don't you?

Christopher: No, I mean self-compassion. Self-compassion is very different from self-esteem.

Wait a minute, I've heard of compassion. To be honest, I don't really know what compassion is, but I've heard that the 14th Dalai Lama is a 'symbol of compassion'. But what on earth is self-compassion? No offence, but that sounds a little bit pretentious to me.

Christopher: No offence taken, but before we delve into the meaning of self-compassion, it might help to differentiate between sympathy, empathy and compassion.

Are you sure you're not trying to dodge my question on self-compassion?

Christopher: Not at all. By becoming clear with respect to sympathy, empathy and compassion, the meaning of self-compassion will be easier to understand.

Fine. I think sympathy means to feel sorry for someone.

Dr Barbara: Yes, I'd go along with that. There's a sense of separateness and it can come across as a bit patronising to the receiver, however well intentioned. "Oh, you poor thing!" Sympathy can be pleasing but can risk being irritating. We also have to ask whether it helps move things forward or digs the hole deeper.

Christopher: Okay, so let's go a step further. What do you understand from the word 'empathy'? What does it mean for you?

Hmm. I'm not quite sure. Does empathy have anything to do with feeling connected to humanity?

Dr Barbara: I'd agree with you. Empathy is actually quite a new word in our vocabulary that has gained traction over the recent decades. The German word, 'einfurlung', was created in the 1930s to capture that sense we have when we really feel like we're in touch with something in an experiential sense. It means to 'feel with'. As this implies, there is that sense of being connected to something or someone. We feel with them. And this shared emotional component is an important aspect of empathy. There is a particular kind of brain cell or neuron in your brain called the mirror neuron, which is partly responsible for this ability we have to feel what someone else is feeling.

Okay, but empathy sounds quite hard, especially if I am to feel what someone else might be feeling.

Dr Barbara: Sometimes, empathy can be hard. When we don't have a common basis of understanding or experience, it can be hard to relate to what someone else is feeling. Our prejudices and judgements can get in the way. At this point, the other aspect of empathy can come into play: the cognitive aspect. This is the ability to think things through, understand what it would be like to be that person, or use our imagination to put ourselves in their position. In this way, we can stretch ourselves to be more empathic, even to people we don't like. This can include ourselves!

So you've explained the difference between sympathy and empathy, but what about compassion and how does this relate to my original question on self-compassion?

Dr Barbara: I will answer your question, I promise. First, I'd just like to say here that all words are representations of concepts. People hear and use the same words differently depending on their own particular experiences, education, upbringing, beliefs, and philosophies.

All words come to mean what they mean by agreement. So people will differ quite a lot in the way they use very conceptual words like empathy and compassion.

I have to admit, for me empathy feels like I'm letting my guard down.

Dr Barbara: A lot of people feel that way, while for others, it's a highly desirable quality. In some people's hands, empathy can be used as a tool for manipulation. Charities, for example, use pictures of suffering children to provoke donations. Adverts aim to get under our skin so we buy products. Generally speaking, though, in my view, empathy is an essential ingredient for social cohesion and something we can do with a lot more of. If we can find common ground with others, we have come a long way, in my view. If we can extend a hand to ourselves, it will ease our pain and promote growth, forgiveness and acceptance.

I always thought empathy was a bit soppy, but I can see that it actually takes courage and creativity to be empathic. And the idea of extending that hand to myself? Hmm, I'll need to think about that!

Dr Barbara: Yes, perhaps the hardest person to make friends with is ourselves. Can we be our own best friend? I often say to people with whom I'm working that the harshest critic you will ever meet is the one you see in the mirror. If we can make friends with ourselves, then we've moved a long way towards healing the need for addictive behaviour.

Where does compassion come into this? Again, for me, that's one of those big 'religious' words that sound a bit wishy-washy and idealistic.

Christopher: In my view, compassion takes empathy to another level. With compassion, there is an internal calling to move empathy into action. Compassion is love in action. For instance, if you have a friend who has called and revealed that they have split up with their partner, to be empathetic would be to imagine what they are feeling and then wish them well.

However, to be compassionate towards your friend means wanting to help them (without wanting to rescue them), perhaps by offering to go for a cup of tea.

Go on…

Christopher: Another part of the process of compassion is a desire to help relieve the suffering of another human being without being attached to an outcome. It's essential that we are not attached to an outcome or result. Otherwise, we miss the opportunity to appreciate the journey and learn from the process. If we try to control results and outcomes, we suffer and become stuck in a cycle of neediness, anxiety and a loss of presence.

That kind of makes sense. Can you explain a bit more about not controlling outcomes? I've been conditioned to believe I can control my results – that I am the master of my fate.

Christopher: No one can control their results. We can, however, control our attitude. When we practise compassion, it is most effective when it is unconditional and free from seeking an outcome – compassion is a matter of choice rather than a self-seeking action. And so, if we assist another human being from a place of presence and compassion, we are not looking to find our happiness off the back of others' suffering. Nor are we trying to control them. Compassion is a conscious choice rather than an emotional knee-jerk reaction.

I'm almost there.

Christopher: If we're attached to an outcome, we cannot be fully present. The foundation of recovery is to operate in the present moment. Whether you are recovering from an addiction or seeking to assist a person professionally or even giving your time to provide a service, it is wise to condition yourself such that you are not emotionally seeking or craving anything from the experience. The 'process' of recovery (learning and reflecting) is the fruit.

This might take some time to fully realise in your consciousness, but if I had to make one suggestion in this dialogue, it is to practise emotionally letting go of outcomes and results.

I sort of understand, but I'll have to come back to this and put time aside to reflect. Although I have been led to believe otherwise, something inside of me is saying that what you have just said is worth investigating.

Dr Barbara: It's hard to get what non-attachment to outcomes actually means. Hard to put into practice and hard to explain! Most people would say, "What's the point if it doesn't make things better?" Let's imagine I'm working with someone or in conversation with them. They may not want to move forward or take on board what I'm saying.

Okay, then what do you do?

Dr Barbara: If I'm attached to an outcome – in other words, have a position that I am right and they must get what I'm saying – I would then be stuck in my own patterns and feelings. At that point, I might feel disappointment or frustration. This would disengage me from being fully present and I would no longer be coming from a place of compassion and connectedness. My desire for a particular outcome would get in the way and potentially block the process for the other person.

So what does work then?

Dr Barbara: I have no right to say what another person's truth is; I can't do that. What I can do is offer space, listen, and be present in a way that hopefully helps the person find their own truth.

I see. What helps you do that?

Dr Barbara: Here comes that word again, 'compassion'. Compassion is a way of being in the world, a verb really. It's a quality from which we choose to operate in life. A way in which there is a really strong desire to be of assistance.

I understand that. I often feel like that, actually, but don't know what to do, so I bury the urge.

Dr Barbara: I believe that the urge to help is natural. We want to relieve the suffering. We recognise the connectedness of all suffering. When we have suffered ourselves and come through that, we realise that crazy things happen to everybody and anybody. There is no judgement or sense of separation. Rather, we feel another's plight as if it could be our own. And, in a way, it is. If we see that it is part of the human condition to struggle and experience hardship, then we experience another's suffering as part of that sea of humanity rather than as specific to them. In that way, we want to do what we can to create better conditions in life for everyone. And here's the really interesting thing about that word 'everyone' – it has to include ourselves!

Oh, I hadn't seen it that way. Of course. If I feel connected to my fellow human beings and recognise that I too am a human being doing the best I can, then of course I'd want the best for myself too! Interesting. I suddenly feel a different relationship to myself: less individualistic, more connected, and more at ease. How interesting.

Dr Barbara: I'm so glad to hear that. And this is exactly what the spirit of compassion brings. We only need to get in touch with the sense of it for our isolation and sense of dis-ease to be relieved. In essence, then, we could argue that we are not actually 'doing' anything. We are creating a way of being. And then, from that space, it becomes natural to want to do what we can to support others in their restlessness and seeking. When we bring this sense of compassion into our dealings with others, it opens up incredible opportunities. There is no judgement, no hierarchy, no power game, no gain or loss – only equality and connection. And yes, love, if I dare introduce that word! 'Love' here meaning a heartfelt connection to another, without agenda.

So, apart from compassion making you feel better, is it actually good for you?

Dr Barbara: Absolutely. Compassion and empathy are two of what are called the 'hive' emotions: ways of being that promote social cohesion. Other hive emotions are kindness, generosity, love, acceptance and forgiveness.

Again, this sounds a bit too biblical to me.

Dr Barbara: Yes, there is that risk, but it's really not about religion. It's about doing what works to promote everyone's happiness and wellbeing. Major religions and wisdom traditions came into being to give us roadmaps for better social functioning. And, interestingly, they all seem to say the same things. Even more interesting to me is that there is now so much scientific evidence to show that human beings are designed to work best, be the healthiest and most fulfilled, when exhibiting behaviours that maximise social cohesion – such as compassion and empathy.

I must admit, I would enjoy my life a lot more if I were to improve my social cohesion.

Dr Barbara: The interesting point to me is that, when we take time every day to sit quietly with ourselves and watch our thoughts rather than get tangled up in them, areas of the brain that relate to empathy and compassion get bigger. By doing something for our own good, we are actually – almost as a sideshow – developing our ability to care for others. I find that fascinating. It brings home the point we made earlier that self-care is an essential first step in supporting others. It's not selfish; it's essential.

So where does self-compassion come into this and what is self-compassion?

Dr Barbara: It is when we remember that taking care of ourselves is an essential step to being able to extend love, warmth, empathy and understanding to others. Our addictive behaviour is often very lonely and comes from a huge sense of separation. We wall ourselves off so that no one can see our behaviour and pain. Self-compassion comes back to realising that we are all in this together, this thing called life, and we all go through our struggles and sufferings. All humans have their battles that they are fighting, their demons within, and their desire to find greater peace. It's a part of life, not singular to ourselves. So we don't need to feel ashamed, guilty, bad or broken.

But what about the things I dislike about myself?

Dr Barbara: Self-compassion works better if we can envelop the things we don't like or want in an attitude of approach rather than of avoidance. Let's approach the question with curiosity. Pushing them away and hating those parts of ourselves doesn't seem to work, so let's try a different approach. Imagine surrounding the parts of ourselves we feel bad about in gentleness, kindness and acceptance. In my experience, this approach releases a lot of the tension and allows us to start moving forward. Then we can begin to entertain the possibility of self-acceptance and move towards self-compassion. As we've seen, this is really compassion for humanity, and we are a part of that great ocean we call humanity.

I'm starting to connect the dots. So self-compassion, in a way, is taking care of myself properly and fully embracing my positive and negative traits?

Christopher: Yes. However, when we practise self-compassion, we look after ourselves just as though we are nurturing a small child. In fact, a major part of grieving our original pain work (so that we can heal and be emotionally liberated) is to re-parent ourselves and reconnect with our inner child. This is what the author, John Bradshaw, meant by 'reclaiming our inner child'. In recovery, we can begin to nurture our inner child and connect deeply with our heart and spirit.

Dr Barbara: I like that image. Often the hurt and blows we receive as children are the source of our addictive behaviour. By embracing our own inner child, we can learn to accept and integrate these parts of ourselves too.

So there's a part of me that is a 'child' even though I am a full-grown adult and if I nurture my inner child, I'll start to heal and grow?

Christopher: Yes, that is possible. I'll share a personal example. My inner child — my spirit — was hurt by a girl I really liked when I was at school. It was really difficult because I was this boy no older than nine, and I had these intense emotions I didn't know what to do with. One day, I plucked up the courage to ask her to be my girlfriend and, to my surprise, she said yes. This was a big deal for a nine-year-old. I was overwhelmed with joy and I was infatuated and walked around the school playground as though I was the king of the land. The following day, just before school ended, she 'dumped me' and immediately found a new boyfriend. I was crushed. A pattern of being guarded and feeling mistrust towards the opposite sex was put in motion at the tender age of nine.

Then what happened?

Christopher: Two years later, at a summer play group for children under twelve, I started to become infatuated with another girl who was similar to the previous girl at middle school. She was very pretty, popular and rebellious. One day, when we were in the playground, she called me a very hurtful thing (a racist comment) in front of the other kids and which I found humiliating. A few weeks later, she said she liked me and she wanted to be my 'girlfriend'. It lasted two days! I therefore started to withdraw even more with respect to being myself around girls and, in later life, women.

Yeah, school infatuations can be hard to live with, but how does this relate to your inner child? And how did you get over that?

Christopher: Well, by the time I was a young teenager, I had grown to distrust girls utterly. I was in a string of seriously dysfunctional 'relationships' and so every time I met a new girl, I put on many masks and shut down. My wounded inner child was badly hurt and so I figured if I hurt them first (on the offensive), I would be safe. I cheated on girls with a warped view that they were going to hurt me anyway, so I'd better 'protect' myself by doing it first. Naturally, this was a recipe for disaster.

I relate to that. My youth was full of circumstances like that. It's really painful. I find trusting really difficult. So how did you get over that? How did you learn to trust again and reconnect with your inner child?

Christopher: It was only when I started to reconnect with my inner child four years into recovery (I was over four years clean and sober off drugs and alcohol) and started to attend a love addiction support group that I was able to trust again and have faith that there are just as many honest and trustworthy women as there are women who are not interested in monogamy. However, it was after ten years of continuous recovery that I started to really dig deep into my childhood grief work and was finally able to reclaim my inner child. I started to take risks again. On a practical level, you can't get very far in this world if you resent and distrust the opposite sex and, sadly, many men and women suffer in this area. Rather than celebrating the opposite sex, they fear them. Empathy and self-compassion has helped me in this area too.

Yeah. I've had problems with the opposite sex for years. But I appreciate you opening up about that. I can see how the inner child work could be useful to me. The problem is that I rarely look after myself properly. I feel embarrassed about saying that.

Christopher: You continuously own up to your masks and addictive patterns, and so you are starting the process of healing. A great quote from the Zen master, Thich Nhat Hahn, summarises self-compassion: "Love is the capacity to take care, to protect, to nourish. If you are not capable of generating that kind of energy towards yourself – if you are not capable of taking care of yourself, of nourishing yourself, of protecting yourself – it is very difficult to take care of another person."

Dr Barbara: It's like on the airplane when they tell parents to put on their own oxygen masks before their child's.

Okay, I'm going to really look into self-compassion, but where do I start?

Christopher: You already have. The next step is to continue to watch out for self-criticism and self-perpetuated struggles.

Struggles? What do you mean by self-perpetuated struggles?

Christopher: It was Dr Barbara who pointed out to me that human beings can also be addicted to struggling, just as we can be addicted to drama or a mind- and mood-altering substance. When we self-perpetuate struggle and attempt to force outcomes, we are not present or in the flow. Dr Barbara?

Dr Barbara: Ah, good point. It's this thing we talked about before regarding being very self-absorbed. That can take over and become an obsession in itself. We can become addicted to fixing ourselves, addicted to some image of ourselves as broken people. We are not broken. We can say "It's okay to be okay" and give up our addiction to the notion that there is something wrong with us. That is a bold and powerful step.

I like that way of seeing it: that these patterns and stories just don't suit us any more.

Dr Barbara: Yes, we need to address these patterns. At the same time, it helps to face outward and look to the needs of others. This is perhaps one of the greatest transformations that can heal us. "He who takes care of the needs of others has already taken care of their own." It's all about balance, isn't it?

I get it. I tend to think that I need to be all 'fixed up' to be a help to others, but you're saying that by placing attention on the care of others, we help ourselves too.

Dr Barbara: Indeed. What if it were like this? First, we need to recognise that there are things we do that perpetuate our pain and understand that these things evolved as our best way to protect ourselves and avoid pain at some point in the past.

Like our addictive behaviours, you mean?

Dr Barbara: Yes. But now these things may have become obsolete. Past their sell-by date. They don't serve us any more.

Okay, include all the 'dodgy' bits rather than think we've got to expurgate them?

Dr Barbara: I like that word! Yes. And then we need to have the courage to let go of our story, who we've been, all the things that damaged us in the past. And live now. In this present moment, the past is in the past and the future is unwritten. We write the future with our current choices. Perhaps the final addiction to let go of is the idea that we are not okay. How does it feel if we say to ourselves, "Right now, I am okay"?

I guess I am okay. I've been trying to fight my way through life for decades, but it has sort of become an adrenalin addiction, if there is such a thing.

Dr Barbara: There absolutely is. In this state, we only feel good when we're 'on the go' and upbeat. Slowing down feels boring, like sinking into the mud. So we keep jacking ourselves up. The problem is, this way, we are always on the run. And it's exhausting. Not just mentally and emotionally, but physically. The constant outpouring of adrenalin is doing huge damage to the internal organs of our body. The constant need for speed means we are never available for others, for listening, for genuine connection. And our brains are firing on overdrive, which creates a sense of rush, time poverty and stress. Why don't we take a pause here?

CHAPTER SEVEN

The treasure trove within

You know what we were talking about earlier? It's just occurred to me that if I'm going to be a compassionate person towards myself, doesn't that mean I'm going to have to be compassionate towards other people?

Christopher: It's true that self-compassion and compassion are deeply integrated, seeing as we are all connected to one another.

I was really hoping you wouldn't say that!

Christopher: Why?

Because with all due respect, I don't want to be compassionate towards everyone. There are loads of people I dislike and a handful of people who have really caused me a lot of harm. I'm sorry, but I cannot be compassionate towards people I dislike!

Dr Barbara: I get that. I know how you feel. For now, let that be. It's really great that you can say those things. Even that is a step forward. Be kind to yourself about this too. Accept that you can't imagine extending compassion to certain people. In fact, in order to say that, you must have already imagined it! Forgiveness is a process and you can't force the bud to open. As you work with being kinder to yourself and as those bits of your brain get stronger, it may happen. When the time is right. You may not feel the way you feel now about these people. You might see it differently. You might feel that you are weighed down by your resentment and anger, and want to be free of them. You might then want to work towards releasing yourself from these unpleasant feelings. After all, the only person those feelings are damaging is you.

Christopher: When we store ill feeling in our minds and bodies, we cannot be happy, peaceful, serene or content. Instead, we will be miserable. And what good is a life that is consumed with bitterness, hostility and resentment? In my own personal recovery, I have found I feel much better when I let go of resentment. Sometimes, it takes time to let go, but it feels so freeing when it happens.

I don't care! Some people have seriously hurt me. Why should I be 'compassionate' towards them? And what about the sick people in the world who kill children or massacre innocent people for the sake of twisted ideologies or politics or just for the fun of it?

Dr Barbara: There are some terrible things happening in the world, it's true. What I can say is that, for my part, my intention is to live in a way that I'm not adding to it. And to be doing what I can to create rivers that flow in a different direction. I have faith in the goodness of humanity. My personal commitment is to do whatever I can to reduce suffering and that includes my own.

I admire you for that, but I have been seriously abused and treated in despicable ways by family members and authority figures in my childhood. My family still mocks me to this day. How can I just let that go?

Christopher: Let's remind ourselves that to be compassionate and forgiving doesn't mean we are endorsing dysfunctional behaviour. On the contrary, it's essential the harm that was inflicted upon us is properly validated and grieved. Forgiveness isn't an intellectual concept or an airy-fairy idea. It's a painstaking process. To be compassionate and to forgive mean we are gradually letting go of poisonous, toxic feelings that are trapped in our minds and bodies.

I just find this very hard to accept, even if I know, in my gut, that what you're saying makes sense.

Christopher: Ill feeling towards oneself or another actually contributes to the collective emotional toxicity in humanity. World War II is a tragic example of what collective bitterness and resentment can do if not properly addressed.

I don't understand.

Christopher: Could a dictator have motivated millions of people to work towards an evil and narcissistic vision if he had been unable to stir up fearful and hateful emotions in them? And so by practising compassion and forgiveness, we heal our wounded self and are actually helping humanity shift into being a more loving and tolerant species.

I agree with you about wars being escalated by ill feeling and greed. It's a horrible fact. And I get the idea that resentment is unhealthy and lethal to my mental health, but it doesn't make it easier. I had a hard childhood, and I have friends who were emotionally, physically and sexually abused while growing up. The idea of forgiving some people makes me boil with incandescent rage.

Dr Barbara: Yes, there is good reason to be angry. Anger can be a great force for change and progress, but not when it's bottled up and held on to. You only damage yourself. And as you work to release the anger you feel about what happened to you, you'll be able to use this forceful sense of injustice to make a difference, rather than have it eat you up from the inside.

I can admit I have problems with anger. I once attended an anger management group, which gave me some good information, but I couldn't shift my rage. And when anyone starts to talk about forgiveness, I start to boil.

Christopher: Anger and particularly inner rage are, more often than not, symptoms of fear. If we look deeper into inner rage, fear is the cause. It's easier to forgive ourselves and be compassionate towards others when we can identify what we are afraid of.

So when I'm angry, I'm actually afraid of something or someone?

Christopher: This is the way I see it. I'd like to suggest the saying 'choose love over fear', as Marianne Williamson would say. And by fear, we are not talking about being aware of, and alert to, real danger. Fear, as I have come to understand it, is a sense of separation from our authentic self and thus separation from everyone else. And when we're lost in fear, addiction can manifest.

I can identify with that. So, looking out for my fears whenever I resist being compassionate will help me to be less angry?

Christopher: Maybe ... try it for yourself. By the way, it's important to point out that forgiveness doesn't mean we have to like the person who has harmed us. In fact, we don't even have to associate with them. What is required from us, however, is to gradually let go of ill feeling. This frees us so we can start to live life again and move on.

Hold on a second. I thought forgiveness meant that you have to bring someone back into your life or even like them?

Dr Barbara: Forgiveness is an internal personal act of moving beyond those feelings for ourselves. The other person may never know. The thing is, whomever we don't forgive has power over us. We're not free. Forgiveness is an act of kindness to ourselves. We are reclaiming lost territory and power.

What about a man I read about in the newspapers who was beaten and sexually abused in a foster care home? How can he get over that? It has stopped him from having healthy relationships with women until he got professional help. My best friend was also raped as a child and it ruined her life. How can they possibly forgive?

Christopher: Naturally, those events are tragic but I cannot talk for them. They might forgive and they might not. However, in order to move on, the emotional attachment to the traumatic event can be healed.

So, emotional healing is possible?

Christopher: I've personally led workshops with men and women who grew up in violent environments and have healed and are contributing to society in a healthy way. If we consider that, up until the 1970s (or around then), it was perfectly acceptable for schoolteachers in England to physically assault pupils for 'punishment' and 'discipline', it would seem that many of us have been abused as children to a certain extent. The point is: we can heal, and by choosing to forgive, we are setting ourselves free.

Dr Barbara: This is the power of human beings. We have a tremendous urge and ability to heal and grow. The patterns laid down in our brains and in our muscles are rewritten daily as we grow. Practising mindful awareness dissolves the unconscious past. Hold on to that powerful intention to break free from the past. In this moment, you are whole and complete. Your story is only present as a memory. When we pull up past memories, the neural pathways that represent them in the brain become somewhat unstable. The connections between the nerve cells loosen a bit. Thus, in that moment, with the right care and attention, there is the possibility to create change. As a result, we can remould, regenerate and reclaim our sense of who we are. Working with skilled and compassionate people in a safe, caring environment has incredible potential to release us. Extending that hand of kindness and forgiveness to ourselves is what we can do, now, to facilitate this process.

What about the kids who bullied me in my childhood and at school? Those memories still haunt me today.

Christopher: It's important to accept that you are still angry at them. Then you might wish to look deeper inside of yourself. Many of us have been bullied. I received my fair share of punches and kicks in school – I was terrified of high school and I was also emotionally bullied by several aggressive teachers, but I've come through that thanks to grieving that hurt in adulthood with friends in recovery and through inner child therapy. Keep in mind that the teenage phase of growing up is harsh and children can also be very cruel. Even the best of us have acted in ways that we wouldn't wish to remember – I was no saint by any stretch of the imagination.

I'm not, by any means, questioning your honesty and I believe you, but how do I actually personally find the strength to forgive and be compassionate?

Dr Barbara: At the end of the day, it's a choice. An act of incredible courage and integrity. When you get in touch with what is possible when you are free of these things, that catalyses the intention. Then we need to 'screw our courage to the sticking point', get support, have faith and jump. The ledge onto which you will land is actually right there under you, and not as far away as it might feel.

Christopher: The first step is to be willing to forgive. If that's too difficult, consider the idea that you might be willing 'to be willing' to practise forgiveness and compassion. We can start to forgive ourselves for our regrettable past behaviour and shameful and guilty memories. Then, when you start to truly forgive yourself for your past addictive patterns and choices, you cannot help but cut other people some slack.

So I'm to start with self-compassion and self-forgiveness?

Dr Barbara: Try it. See what happens. See it as an experiment and be curious about the results. I can't dictate to you what will work for you. All I can offer is my own experience of what worked for me, and what seems to work for others.

Okay. I'll give this a try, but I'm still feeling self-doubt.

Dr Barbara: These are lofty topics in one way. In another way, they are physical realities that create cascades of chemicals in our brain and body that build an upward cycle of wellbeing. When we try it for a little bit, we immediately realise how beneficial it is. This encourages us to proceed. We are literally re-programming the addictive patterns in the reward centres of our brain. The rush of wellbeing from realising a moment of self-compassion brings its own reinforcing rewards. Once we get a glimpse of that, it gets so much easier. An upwards spiral is generated. We start to feel honest and clean in relating to others. It's a relief not to be on the run and hiding. Our relationships improve. We notice these things, and this motivates us to not break the bottom line.

I mean, I'm not saying I'm an angel, by any means. I've caused my fair share of harm to others over the years. I suppose I would like the people I care about to forgive me too. I don't know why I got so defensive when you both started talking about compassion and forgiveness.

Christopher: That's okay. I also used to get defensive when people suggested practising forgiveness and compassion because it felt as if they were diminishing all of the hurt and pain I had experienced. Then, one day, after grieving the big chunks of my original pain work, I acknowledged that I had caused a lot of people pain due to my own addictive patterns of behaviour and so, if I wanted others to forgive me, it would be dishonest not to forgive others.

So I guess I make an intention to practise self-compassion and forgiveness?

Christopher: Yes. We always start with an intention.

Dr Barbara: The intention to be well, to heal and to grow is innate. When you cut your finger, it heals without you even having to pay attention to it. It's natural. It's great for us to remind ourselves of that, and get in touch with the awareness that we are a part of nature. There is a natural force inside you that wants to heal, grow and move forward. Think of how the young child's growth and development happens automatically, from birth, to sitting, crawling, standing, walking, talking. So too does the growth of our inner world and consciousness. We can come to trust that. Keep reminding and asking yourself at every step, "What is my intention here?" Our intentions generate our actions, attitudes and where we place our attention. By reminding yourself of the intention to heal, you are catalysing powerful shifts inside yourself.

Thank you. I will explore compassion and see where it takes me. I feel a bit stronger. This is definitely doable. And definitely worth doing.

Dr Barbara: Thank you!

CHAPTER EIGHT

Patterns

Although I'm starting to see things differently about myself and addiction, I still have a few things on my mind.

Christopher: What's on your mind?

I don't think that I'm the only addict in my family. My uncle and grandfather were both alcoholics and my family is very dysfunctional. My sister has many more addictive issues than me and she is probably a sex and love addict too. She attracts men who are incapable of having relationships or are married.

Christopher: I wish your family well and especially your sister. It sounds like she might be suffering from emotional anorexia, which many sex and love addicts and codependents suffer from.

There you go again, confusing me with mind-boggling concepts. What do you mean by 'emotional anorexia'? Everyone knows that anorexia is an eating disorder!

Christopher: In the addiction recovery community, we recognise that addicts can starve themselves of receiving social, sexual or emotional nourishment. Sex and love addicts starve themselves of a healthy, personal relationship and, consequently, deliberately avoid wholesome relationships with other human beings. We're getting quite deep now, but there are many papers and books published on sexual and emotional anorexia. I have also suffered from emotional anorexia. It's no myth!

That's left me flabbergasted. So if my sister has this, I probably have this too. How is sexual and emotional anorexia defined? Is this prompting me to act out and strengthen my addiction?

Christopher: Think of a sex and love addict who refuses to have a wholesome relationship with themselves and denies themselves emotional intimacy, vulnerability and openness with other human beings. This causes suffering because we are social creatures. In other words, as mentioned in the Augustine Fellowship, "Anorexia is the compulsive avoidance of giving or receiving social, sexual, or emotional nourishment."

Blimey! Well, I certainly have been starving myself of intimacy and authenticity. I know my sister has too. She is in a lot of pain but puts on a brave face and comes across as super confident. She is a powerhouse in her industry! I don't want to divert from my own addiction but I am worried about her.

Christopher: Love addicts often pick partners who are emotionally unavailable because deep down, they don't feel worthy of having a healthy, loving relationship. A love addict craves and obsesses about becoming enmeshed or 'one' with another human being at all costs, even if it means putting themselves in potential danger.

What are their addictive behaviours like? Do love addicts have certain patterns?

Christopher: They might use emotional blackmail, threaten to kill themselves, plead, bribe or compulsively commit adultery to get the attention of their partner – they believe their relationship can fill an empty void, which is impossible. Underneath this compulsion are often grave abandonment issues, childhood trauma and a fear of intimacy.

I get the whole 'abandonment issues' thing. My parents were at work most days and rarely made me feel accepted as a child – I know it had an effect on my sister. But what about my codependent family and why are their addictive patterns different from my sister and I?

Christopher: Love addiction and codependency are different. However, a human being can suffer from both. A codependent finds it almost impossible to protect their boundaries with others (or respect other people's boundaries) and finds it difficult to differentiate their own values. They have to be in control and/or they allow people to control them utterly.

My family has a lot of denial around this, and that's what has made it very hard for me to come to terms with my own addiction. From the outside looking in, my family appears to be successful but behind closed doors, there's so much anger and rage. It's awful!

Christopher: Yes, that is a common trait in codependent families. A codependent will resent the people they control or who control them. They can easily make someone a 'demigod' and therefore neglect their own opinions and values. For instance, a codependent might date someone to try and change them, to 'fix' them – a new project to stop them looking at their own unresolved addiction. Melody Beattie and Pia Mellody have written great material on this subject.

That rings true to me. I can also see that in my family. My aunt became a carer to my alcoholic uncle.

Christopher: Yes, codependents make great 'rescuers' but it often leads to greater suffering. Have you heard of the Karpman drama triangle?

I can't say that I have. What is it?

Christopher: The Karpman drama triangle is a classic model of codependent behaviour. First of all, a codependent will rescue someone. Then, when their 'brave and charitable' work hasn't been acknowledged, they become very angry at the person they have attempted to rescue. And finally, they start to feel like a victim. They feel sorry for themselves and complain how the person they rescued never appreciated them. The important thing to learn here is that if a person wants to change, it's because they have made a decision to do so.

Dr Barbara: That's a really important point. We look at other people and think, "Well, they're as bad as me or worse, so why should I bother to change?" Or we might think, "They are the ones to blame. They need to change for me to be well."

Ultimately, the only person we can change is ourselves. And the only way to find our freedom is to look inside ourselves. It comes back to that word 'responsibility'. Responsibility and acceptance go hand in hand. The first step is to accept the way things are. The second step is to give up blame, resentment and bitterness towards others.

I have always blamed my toxic relationships on the other person. Until this dialogue, I've never thought to really take responsibility for my part in relationships. What else can I do about this?

Dr Barbara: What works is to say to oneself, "Okay, this is how it is. I have addictive behaviours. And it's hundred per cent up to me to move beyond this, regardless of anyone or anything else." We can't blame the circumstances, other people, the weather – any of it. When we take responsibility, we start to have power. That power generates commitment. And that commitment catalyses change.

That's so powerful. So, by accepting and fully conceding that I have a problem with addiction, I can begin to gain power and heal my life? I'm starting to see a lot of things now. I guess my denial regarding myself and family is starting to diminish.

Christopher: Yes. Many of us in recovery, including scores of addiction rehabs, would agree that addiction is a family condition or illness. If one family member is an untreated drug addict, alcoholic or codependent, their dysfunctional behaviour starts to eat away at the remaining family members. It creates resentment, financial insecurities and emotional agony.

Yes, I can see the logic behind that. I suppose it's like the domino effect.

Christopher: Think of an untreated sex addict who spends hours every night until the early hours watching pornography on the internet instead of spending that time with their wife or husband, and then becomes so tired due to the late nights that their professional life suffers. The sex addict's behaviour will cause resentment, destroy trust and create economic insecurities in the family and home.

I've never thought about it like that.

Christopher: A sex addict is also emotionally anorexic – they must be in order to continue participating in isolated behaviour such as being addicted to pornography and being promiscuous or having multiple affairs. All of these secretive behaviour patterns affect a family and home.

Dr Barbara: Realising that we are part of a larger pattern of maladjusted behaviour within a family system can come as a bit of a shock.

You are not wrong there!

Dr Barbara: As we grow up, our reality is generated and framed for us by the people closest to us. As children, we have idealised versions of the people who are our carers and parents in our internal world view. This is natural when you consider that these people are our security and our source of love, shelter and survival.

Yes, that certainly rings true for me.

Dr Barbara: Our main carers also act as models for our development. We can even idolise dysfunctional parents and wish to be like them. As we mature, it can be shocking to come to see people the way they actually are and realise that they are also human, with dysfunctional behaviour and beliefs we don't share or even condone.

I can see how that can lead to a lot of antipathy, even hatred if we blame these people.

Dr Barbara: A lot of family constellations break down irrevocably, sadly. I think it's useful to understand that the separation process between parent and child is part of growing, part of becoming our own person, with our own values, personalities and sense of who we are. Then we can reconnect, adult to adult. Unless, of course, our parents insist on staying in the parent role.

That keeps them stuck too, though.

Dr Barbara: Yes, it does, but we can't force people to change. All we can do is be open and honest about ourselves. Sometimes that is enough to catalyse a shift on the other side. We have to let go of blame, shame and guilt. Seeing the flaws in our family system can help us understand how we got where we are. And then we must choose, as adults wishing to be well, how we want to proceed. It can feel like a kind of shedding as we move forward and let go of the 'self' that was shaped unconsciously by our past.

I get that. I find it very hard to be true to myself. I don't even know who I am, to be perfectly honest. Until this conversation, I thought I was someone else. Now I just don't know any more. What has always baffled me is that my aunt and uncle are social hermits. Both of their fathers were alcoholics but they aren't alcoholics. But they behave in similar ways to their parents. Again, they would be considered decent members of society, but withdraw from anyone outside of their immediate family.

Christopher: That's what the addiction field or the twelve-step community calls 'isms' (family dysfunction).

What on earth are 'isms'?

Christopher: 'Isms' are described as transference of addictive patterns of dysfunctional behaviour, passed down from generation to generation. For instance, if a mother was an alcoholic who never made it into recovery, her behaviour would leave a mark on her children, husband, etc. Unless her adult children join some sort of recovery programme and adopt the mindfulness practice, they will have very similar behaviour traits to their mother but minus the alcohol abuse. There is a strong possibility that they will become codependent and form relationships with other codependents or alcoholics.

Yeah. That makes sense but is there any scientific evidence to support that?

Dr Barbara: The child's brain is moulded by its experiences. Important neural pathways are laid down in the early years of life, especially those that process emotion. It would take a very self-aware child to not soak up the patterns, beliefs and behaviours of their carers. And this learnt patterning gets passed down the generations, unless someone says, "Stop! I am going to create another possibility for myself."

Was this the case with your family?

Dr Barbara: In my family, emotions were highly suppressed, especially anger. We presented the image of the perfect middle-class upwardly mobile family. I learnt a great deal from my parents that I am very grateful for. My mum was super-organised, patient and very gentle. My dad had determination and drive and a great sense of humour. I internalised these qualities. I also internalised a strong sense that if anything was wrong, it should be buried, pushed away, and denied. As a result, I developed a kind of emotional favouritism. It was okay to be happy, but not okay to be sad, angry or fearful. It was not okay to not succeed, to express self-doubt or want to live outside of the tight reality that was our family system. The only way I could find my way out of this compacted situation was to smash my way out. To rebel, reject, disconnect and run. I caused my parents a lot of pain. Once 'free' – or that's what it felt like – I started to find my own way, learn how to make friends with all my feelings and find ways to express myself authentically. I see this as an ongoing learning process.

So how have things worked out with your family?

Dr Barbara: At some point, it became possible for me to be strong enough in my own reality to re-enter the family orbit. It was very challenging, as those deep-seated behaviour patterns would get reactivated as soon as I stepped over the threshold of their front door. There was a lot of dysfunctional conditioning within the whole family constellation. With greater self-awareness and patience, I was able to stay true to myself, and slowly rebuild my relationship with each of my parents, adult to adult.

Wasn't that hard though? I mean, how long did it take you to rebuild your personal relationships?

Dr Barbara: It took many, many years and a lot of love and commitment. With my father, it only really happened a few days before he died. He had 'excommunicated' me for marrying a man with a different skin colour.

Goodness – he was racist?

Dr Barbara: Yes. I also had to realise that I couldn't change my parents. I had to learn to accept them and love them exactly the way they were. I apologised for the damage I had done and the lack of gratitude I had felt. I realised that they had done their very best and loved me. Looking back through their childhood, I came to understand how they had become the way they were. I could put myself in their shoes and this sowed the seeds of compassion.

Christopher? What about you?

Christopher: I had to come clean about my addiction to drugs and alcohol. To be honest, my family already knew I had a problem with alcohol and drugs during my teenage years. It certainly wasn't a secret. It's been a long and slow process of healing. It took a while for my family to see that the untreated addiction was behind me. My parents were very supportive, but I had to do the work – ask for help and take responsibility for my recovery.

And does your family respect your boundaries?

Christopher: Well, it's interesting that you put it like that. Yes, they do, but it took time for them to adjust to my way of living as a person in recovery. I don't see it as something to be ashamed of. But I've come to realise, as an adult who is years into recovery, that I don't have to carry the burden of toxic shame that previous generations had to live with. And I certainly cannot change my family. It took a long time to fully accept this.

Do they respect that you have to be true to yourself?

Christopher: Well, yes. But it took time. I had to rebuild my life from scratch – mentally, emotionally, physically, spiritually, socially and economically, which didn't happen overnight. Then I realised that I had emotional boundaries. I learnt to listen carefully to my intuition and gut. It was a painstaking process, getting my family to understand that my emotional boundaries were not to be broken. I also had to learn to respect their space and to not impose myself on their boundaries. This is a process into healthy adulthood.

I'm starting to sense that there are no shortcuts in long-term recovery or that I can't get away with cutting corners. I feel the impatience in me wanting to get everything done now but I see it doesn't work like that.

Dr Barbara: I do believe that, as each generation stands on the shoulders of the one before, it is possible to create healthier relationships. As each of us become more self-aware, we make it possible for our children to grow up with a greater sense of who they are and how to be true to that. My children are far more switched on to loads of this stuff than I am. My intention has always been that they learn from my mistakes and have the freedom to find their own way.

Christopher: That's wonderful news.

Yes, it is. So how do I get the balance though? I mean, I need to have boundaries but, at the same time, I still want to be kind and friendly. I want to learn how to be assertive but not feel guilty for being that way.

Christopher: In my opinion, being kind to ourselves means we protect ourselves and do not allow ourselves to be used or abused. We can work on our self-worth every day.

What do you mean?

Christopher: Not too long ago, I had to inform a company that I would take them to court for not paying me for services rendered. I was subsequently on the receiving end of some very unpleasant emails, attacking me personally. But I refused to back down, as I knew that I had not put a foot wrong with regard to the services and products they received from me and that they were simply trying to shirk their financial responsibilities. I took counsel from my partner, business mentor, lawyer and my peer group, and they all agreed that the company was behaving unethically and so I informed them that I would take legal action. I am pleased to say that this worked and they paid me the sum of money that was owed to me.

But doesn't that go against being spiritual? I mean, you openly talk about forgiveness. You've just shared the importance of kindness and compassion. Aren't you contradicting yourself?

Christopher: No. I behaved with integrity and stood my ground. I would have been cheating myself if I hadn't.

Didn't you feel bad about the situation? Wouldn't you feel guilty about that? I know I feel guilty whenever I have to be confrontational or am in the midst of conflict.

Christopher: Many of us can feel guilty about doing what's right for us. This is another symptom of low self-worth and a lack of mindfulness. We fear people not loving and accepting us for our choices, even if our choices resonate with our heart and spirit. As long as we are certain that we are behaving with integrity, we need not fear taking a firm course of action, no matter how far out of our comfort zone this takes us.

I need to work on my sense of self-worth. It's an area that has ruined my chances of living a happy life.

Christopher: Tragically, many people allow others to walk all over them because they feel that if they stand up for themselves, they aren't being kind or 'spiritual'. And as we have discussed in this dialogue, kindness is only authentic when we direct it towards ourselves first.

Dr Barbara: There is a big difference between being kind and being nice.

I've never thought about it like that. I was starting to think I had to be some kind of martyr or doormat – to stay in my people-pleaser role.

Christopher: Another thing to watch out for is that many recovering love addicts and codependents feel guilty when people do them harm. They take on the toxic shame and guilt of the people doing the harmful deeds. I made up my mind some time ago to not let that happen to me. Even when I feel myself carrying other people's toxic shame and guilt (for their undesirable behaviour), I quickly release that toxicity from my consciousness.

So we can stand up for ourselves and by doing so, we're being kind? We don't have to let people walk over us even if we practise kindness and mindfulness?

Dr Barbara: On the contrary, standing firm in ourselves and our own integrity is paramount. This doesn't mean being unkind, harsh or difficult. It simply means talking clearly and calmly about the way we see things and what we know to be true. When we do this, it has profound effects. It allows others to speak their truth and move forward. Otherwise, we are participating in a dance of deception that just goes nowhere, busy being 'nice' to cover our own – excuse the word – backsides!

Christopher: When all is said and done, we enter this world alone and we leave it alone. If we can look at ourselves in the mirror before we retire at night and know that we haven't allowed anyone to attempt to dent our self-worth, we'll be just fine.

Dr Barbara: Or they may have attempted to do that, but we saw it for what it was and didn't buy into it. There is no need to create anger or resentment inside ourselves when this happens. Just acknowledge, and then let it go.

That's very reassuring.

Christopher: Remember that no matter how kind we are to ourselves and others, we'll still be in conflict with some people, even if we have no desire to be. Conflict is part of the human journey and is sometimes unavoidable, but we can meet it with integrity and dignity.

Dr Barbara: Conflict is part of life. Think of how boring it would be without it. We don't need to fear it but embrace it, welcome the creative cauldron it generates and trust ourselves.

And I suppose developing self-worth and self-kindness will ultimately lead to a balanced and fulfilling life?

Dr Barbara: As you become more self-aware, more in tune with what you are feeling, and more able to stay true to your own experience, you are revitalising your emotional intelligence. As you get stronger in a sense of yourself, it gets easier to stay balanced. You more quickly notice when you lose your internal reference point, that sense of being connected to your own reality. This means that you are less likely to be pulled off course by others' behaviours, feelings and reactions.

From this centre of calm, you can be true to your higher ideals of being kind and friendly without surrendering your inner world and reality. Imagine that you have a strong inner core, a place that you can come back to, a home inside of yourself that is always there. Notice when you are not 'at home'. Bring yourself back by taking a moment out. Press pause. Give yourself a breathing space to rebalance, recalibrate and reconnect.

I'm still afraid of not being able to maintain my boundaries without being unkind or neglecting my family. It sounds like a tall order.

Christopher: To stay true to ourselves and remain kind to others is an art. It does require daily vigilance and, at the same time, it's important to remember that art can often get messy. Whenever we set an emotional boundary, we can express this to our families and friends in a clear, strong and appropriate way that maintains a sense of respect and love (but in a tone that is not aggressive). It doesn't mean we don't love them any more. We are just taking care of our wellbeing. We are also showing them that it's possible for them to have boundaries too.

What if they dismiss my boundaries? I'm afraid that I'll rage at them. I get really angry when I feel people do not understand me.

Christopher: When you start to assert certain boundaries to protect yourself, you may come up against resistance. Your family and friends may become angry, bad-mouth you, plead with you, attempt to convince you that 'you've been brainwashed', etc. Or they might completely lose themselves in codependent behaviour. You'll be going against the grain and if you're the only one in recovery, expect resistance.

But what if they never change their ways?

Dr Barbara: They may not. I think it's important to realise this going in. And ask yourself if this is okay. They may not change. Can you accept this and keep on your own path anyway?

At the moment, I'm not sure if I can fully accept that my loved ones won't change. I am open to it though.

Dr Barbara: Remember that this is your journey. You can make it without them changing, approving, supporting or even knowing about it. We have to make choices. Sometimes, these choices look harsh. Keep your eye on the target. Keep compassion and kindness firmly on your horizon. As long as your intention is to do no harm, your road will be full of friends.

Christopher: Sometimes, however, a family member might decide to investigate what recovery is but, more than likely, they won't. If they are relatively young, they have a better chance because their habits aren't so entrenched. Having said that, I personally know two brave men who addressed their addictions in their late sixties and early seventies. For me, they are among the bravest of us.

Dr Barbara: That is really amazing. It's never too late. A patient of mine got themselves to the other side of twenty-six years of bulimia. I have so much respect for this courage and determination to be free, to commit to another way and to create a new range of possibilities for their life. Every moment is precious. There is only this moment.

I've gained a lot of hope from this conversation. You've given me a lot to reflect on.

CHAPTER NINE

The long and winding road leads me home…

Up until today, I've seen getting better as climbing some impossibly enormous mountain. A mountain with slippery slopes and crevices to fall into. And that thought alone has stopped me from even setting foot on the road, let alone the mountain. What you guys seem to be saying is that healing is a natural force within me. And that there is only now, this moment. So if I can be present to what I'm thinking and feeling in this moment now, and accept that with kindness and gentleness towards myself, that's it. And so I just need to keep being 'in the moment', one step at a time.

Dr Barbara: That's brilliant! What a long way we've come since the start of this conversation. And ... as we've mentioned, it's not always easy. So we need to put in place structures, both metaphorical and tangible structures, as safety nets to catch us when we fall, and as guide rails so we know we're on the right track when the fog descends. And you can be sure that there will always be days when the fog descends.

What would you recommend? Any suggestions?

Christopher: Healthy and non-shaming mirroring is an important part of the process. We can gain this from a highly emotionally intelligent and effective peer group that has our best interests at heart.

What do you mean by that? A support network?

Christopher: When we were children, we used to look for approval or consent from those closest to us. For instance, a two-year-old baby boy might look at his father before picking up an object from a shelf to see what facial expression he gets (hopefully, his father didn't rage or shame the child). However, as we grow up and evolve into our authentic selves, our mirroring from family members can be distorted. And so, if we have a peer group that resonates with the vision we have for ourselves, life becomes a lot easier to process.

My peer group certainly doesn't have my best interests at heart. Most of my peer group is based around work and if they had a chance to screw me over to climb the ladder, I have no doubt they would.

Christopher: That's why it's important to choose your friends wisely and make sure they support your vision, mission, purpose and hold you accountable to take action every day and enjoy the journey.

Dr Barbara: People who will be kind, not nice!

Yeah, I need to start meeting emotionally intelligent people. I could do with having friends who actually understand what I'm going through and who have my best interests at heart. I feel a little bit more confident this is possible now.

Christopher: Fellowship is essential. It means we can make regular phone calls, send emails or go for a cup of tea or coffee with friends in recovery and reconnect and share our humanness, instead of isolating ourselves and silently suffering. This is why support groups such as the twelve-step fellowships (for people who prefer a spiritual approach) and therapy secular groups (for people who prefer a therapeutic approach) have helped millions of people recovering from addiction.

Dr Barbara: The support of others who really know what it's like and the tricks our minds can play is immensely valuable. You are not alone. Find workshops, retreats, or groups. Build a network of trusted associates, people you know you can count on to keep you true to your bottom line.

Thanks. That's very helpful. So what else do you recommend?

Dr Barbara: I found that I had a lot of weeding and pruning to do in my life, to create an environment that supported me in moving forward.

How did that take shape?

Dr Barbara: As my conscious awareness of life became clearer (by practising mindfulness every day and meditating), I started to see things, people and patterns of behaviour in ways that I'd been blind to before. I could see that certain people, who seemed perfectly fine on the outside, did not actually have my best interests at heart. In some cases, it was as if they had an investment in keeping me small and stuck.

So then what?

Dr Barbara: I had to make some tough choices about how to live and who to allow into what I call my 'inner circle'. The people I knew I could really trust to be honest, straightforward and loving. I found that these qualities in relationships were a function of communication. Love is a function of communication. As soon as things go unsaid, they swirl around in our head and create distance between people.

I do that a lot. And it can really destroy friendships.

Dr Barbara: We all do it. It's an ongoing job to keep the space 'clean', as it were. People in my inner circle are all people with whom I know there is honesty and respect. We clear up misunderstandings as quickly as we can. We don't let things fester. And we strive to see the best in each other, to speak to the human being, not the garbage that we can all sometimes present as who we are.

That strikes a chord in a big way with me. I'm not sure I have many of those types of friends. I might end up very lonely.

Dr Barbara: You won't. As you weed and prune, you create space for new things to come into your life. And as you are coming from a place of greater integrity and light within yourself, you attract good things to you. The thing is to cultivate good habits within yourself and have the intention to be the best person you can be. This is a continuous existential challenge. In each moment, we have a choice about which way to face – towards the dark side or towards the light. The more we choose to turn to the light, the easier that choice becomes. We can actively build new habits that serve us.

Is that what you mean when you talk about taking responsibility for your life?

Dr Barbara: Yes. It means being the active participant in creating how your life is and who you choose to be. People ask, "How can I find myself?" A more powerful question is, "Who do I choose to be? Who can I create myself as, right now?" There is no 'you' to find. There is only this moment and the choices you make. Mindful meditation on a daily basis is a skill that I highly recommend you cultivate. It allows you to have greater sense of space and choice in your life. It is a gift you are giving yourself, taking the time to spring-clean your thoughts on a daily basis, to return to solid ground, a place of stillness and tranquillity. As you build the habit of finding this 'home inside yourself', it becomes easier to locate that sense of yourself when the going gets tough. It is also a very powerful way to create changes in the way your brain works.

I get that.

Dr Barbara: By spending ten to fifteen minutes a day with a strong intention to bring the focus of your attention to your breath, you are exercising mind muscles that alter the substrate of your brain. The brain changes in ways that improve your sense of wellbeing, how your immune system works, your motivation, your ability to understand what you are feeling. And, as we discussed earlier, it is so important to be in touch with your emotions. The inability to feel what you're feeling when you feel it feeds addictive behaviour and keeps us stuck. Indeed, the need to run from our feelings lies behind a lot of self-destructive behaviour. Putting aside a short amount of time every day to practise being in touch with yourself, with an attitude of kindness and curiosity, is a very simple yet powerful practice. You start to see things more clearly. The fog starts to lift and you realise what needs to be done to spring-clean your life.

I would love to see things more clearly, rather than through my messy and addictive perceptions. I suppose I have more thinking to do.

Christopher: Remember that we cannot think our way out of addiction – we can only act our way out of addiction. And by this, I mean taking small steps, one day at a time, in the present moment, to change our habits. Powerful questions to ask each morning are, "How can I serve without being attached to an outcome?" or "How can I serve without letting my desires and emotions control me?" or "How can I sufficiently re-parent myself?" The answers will come. And then, it is our responsibility to act on those answers.

They are very helpful suggestions but I feel that pretty much every corner of my life has skeletons in it. That's a bit daunting.

Dr Barbara: This is where kindness towards yourself comes in again. And patience. Things take time. Be patient. Take small steps that feel safe. Make sure you have at least one person you can trust as a point of reference for the life you are building for yourself. Make sure you see that person regularly and speak honestly with them. Allow yourself to be supported and accept that support. Let it in.

I'm still afraid of my 'skeletons' though. How can I attract new supportive friends if I have skeletons?

Christopher: 'Skeletons' are emotions, memories, sensations and suppressed grief. You can address them in a sane way through the aid of a recovery programme, fellowship, mindfulness and professional help. You don't need to be dominated by your fears any more. As the author, Susan Jeffers, wrote: "Feel the fear and do it anyway."

I'm willing to make a positive change in my life. I can already feel the resistance though.

Christopher: When we release our fears and feel connected to another human being or a group of emotionally intelligent people, when we meditate regularly and see how we can contribute to life in our own way, we are in the flow of recovery. The fear you are feeling will gradually dissolve.

So what I'm really getting from all of this is that change comes from within rather than from outside of myself.

Dr Barbara: Absolutely. It's not so much about changing the external circumstances of one's life, although sometimes this is necessary. It's more about the inner landscape. Fill your inner landscape with peaceful, inspiring things. Cultivate peace on the inside. Get into the habit of being generous. With your time, with your love, with compliments and actions. At the beginning of the day, create one main intention for that day. "Today, my intention is to be generous." "Today, my intention is to be kind to myself." Write it down. Writing things down makes them stick better in our awareness. When we write something down, we are about nine times more likely to carry it through.

I like that idea. So I'm literally creating my day. Oh, actually my future! I get it!

Dr Barbara: Exactly! And then, at the end of the day, write down three things that went well that day. Scan through the day and, no matter what your opinion is about how it went, find three things that went well. Some days, it can feel like just brushing your teeth was an achievement! Other days, everything seems to flow with real ease and effortlessness.

That's very helpful. Do you have anything else you can suggest?

Dr Barbara: Ask yourself who was the source of these things going well. Start shifting your gaze from what's wrong to what works. Soon you will notice that the critical gaze you have on yourself is starting to soften, and you are able to see the good in yourself. It feels like coming home. Coming home to where you started. I really like that great line by T. S. Eliot: "We shall not cease from explorations. And the end of all our exploring will be to arrive where we started and know the place for the first time."

Christopher: I personally write a letter of gratitude before I retire at night (most nights). Even if I have had a difficult day, I still write. Sometimes, gratitude has to be cultivated and, at other times, it flows effortlessly. The main thing is that I write regardless of how I am feeling. I also journal, which is very cathartic. In the morning, I put one hour aside to settle the mind through mindfulness, meditation, yoga, reading spiritual literature and connecting with my Higher Power. I also put time aside to silently wish people well (prayer) and visualise my dreams and goals.

That's very inspiring. Did you two seek help on your journey?

Dr Barbara: Yes, and I found it quite challenging to find the right people, to be honest – people who didn't judge, categorise and label me as broken. Who you are can never be broken. I wanted support that empowered me to be me, rather than fix me. I knew somewhere deep inside that I wasn't broken. I just needed the right guidance and perspective, a perspective that saw the journey of human life as just that – a journey. I wanted to feel accepted, that whoever I was with really wanted to bring out the best in me and had the space to hold my pain without judgement. I definitely recommend finding a trusted mentor, a professional person you have a good rapport with.

I have professional mentors for business but this dialogue is so deep and personal. I mean, how on earth do I find a trusted mentor that I can share my emotions with? That's a daunting prospect.

Dr Barbara: You'll know whether they are the right person for you or not. You might need to shop around. It might just be for a while, but it's hard to walk this road on your own.

I think I have a belief system that says that we're supposed to be able to make it on our own.

Dr Barbara: Yes, I had that too. That's one thing I realised in learning to be kind to myself: it's okay, if not essential, to ask for help. In fact, it's a sign of strength. There were a few key people who came into my life once I'd determined to be well. I went to see a counsellor for a while. I learnt how to reach out for help.

I guess there are a few people I can count on.

Dr Barbara: Glad to hear that. A couple of my friends turned out to be true friends too.

I guess the proof of the pudding will be in the eating.

Dr Barbara: Certainly. You know people by their actions. My children were my motivating force. I was determined for us to heal as a family. I got much better at saying no when I needed to, and asking myself how I felt about things before rushing in. I took time out to slow down, take each day as it comes, and I stopped pushing myself. It meant losing the security of a pay cheque at the end of every month. But I realised that the health and happiness of the people I loved most and, of course, my own, were of far greater value than any material wealth.

That is so true.

Dr Barbara: The decisions I made and the steps I took kind of made themselves once I allowed myself to let go and trust that I could and would heal. Mostly, I learnt to forgive myself. I learnt to be kind to me. I placed my attention on the needs of others, and this helped the healing process. It's a fine balance between needing to look inside oneself to sort things out and not getting so self-absorbed that it becomes narcissistic.

That has given me a lot of hope. What about you, Christopher? What help did you receive?

Christopher: I certainly sought help and I continue to do so. Like Dr Barbara, through trusted mentors and friends, I learnt to balance self-compassion and being of service to others. I too took time off work. When I hit rock bottom in late summer 2004, I was still working as a DJ. I took three months off from DJing to give my mind and body a rest, and fellowship with people in recovery. Not everyone needs to take a long break from work. Many people I know who are in recovery did not find it necessary to do so, but they all required professional and spiritual help. I have also found original pain work therapy or counselling to be incredibly powerful and liberating.

I'm really taking on board what you're saying. I want to start now!

Dr Barbara: Yes, now is the time to start. Buy yourself a good notebook to write in at the beginning and end of every day. Start writing a journal. Keep a record of your journey. I did this and it is amazing to look back and see where I was and where I am now. Also, writing things down really helps to clear out some of the junk we've got in our own mental attic. All those thoughts and memories. Get them out of your head and down on paper. It helps us process stuff, let go and move on.

Great idea. And you're right. I used to write a journal. I find writing things down helps me put things in perspective and see things differently. And I find it relaxing too. I just don't give myself time to do it any more.

Dr Barbara: We all need to realise that prioritising time for self-care is paramount and actually makes us more effective when we are at work.

That's true. I tend to get less and less productive the longer I work. I come back refreshed if I 'indulge' in a short break.

Dr Barbara: The next thing to do is to find a place in your home that you can make into a quiet place. It need only be a corner or a special chair. Make this space lovely, maybe with a plant or picture, and keep it clean and simple. What you are creating is a place where you can go to feel free, to be you on your own, to sit and focus on your breath. A place to watch your thoughts go by without getting sucked into them. Can you think of a spot at home you could turn to your 'quiet' corner?

Yep. I know just the spot.

Dr Barbara: Now make a firm contract with yourself to go to this place once a day. Pick a time in the day that works for you and write it in your diary and/or on your smart phone. Set a reminder. See this as an important appointment with yourself. It is really important. What could be more important than your own wellbeing? Then make sure you keep that appointment with yourself every day.

This sounds great! I'm all set up. But, hang on, I know me. What if I slip off the wagon and start getting up to my usual nonsense?

Dr Barbara: Once you've taken the time out a few times, you will feel so much benefit that you will be motivated to keep it up. And if you fall off the wagon, just get back on it. Don't bash yourself up and go into a big guilt trip about it. That's part of the racket you're giving up. Be firm and kind to yourself. You're developing self-discipline. Remind yourself of your intention. Look and see where and what the triggers were that took you off your path. Learn from that and move on with that learning tucked under your belt. The next time similar triggers occur, you'll have greater knowledge and self-awareness of the mechanisms behind how you sabotage yourself. As you develop this mindful self-awareness, it will get easier to catch yourself before the automatic responses kick in and take over.

I feel that that is going to be one of the hardest habits to change: beating myself up. I've spent most of my life obsessing about my mistakes. However, I do feel hopeful now and I sense what you're saying is true. I'm up for the journey.

Christopher: The worst thing to do after a relapse is to beat yourself up. Relapse in any addictive pattern of behaviour is a result of old addictive thoughts and emotions left to fester. For instance, take the recovering codependent. She has a strong recovery that keeps her from craving to control people. Then, after a year of sound practice, she stops taking the action that got her mentally, emotionally and spiritually grounded. She lets her mind dominate her. Consequently, she reverts back to trying to control everyone in sight. The relapse – breaking addictive, bottom-line behaviour – was a result of neglecting a practice that previously worked for her.

I guess mindful self-awareness would be able to detect any thoughts that suggest neglecting my recovery?

Christopher: Exactly. Addictive patterns start to play out in the mind before they manifest in our behaviour. The art is to remain vigilant and to go with the flow. This sounds like a contradiction to the intellectual mind. However, when we start to operate in the present moment, remaining vigilant and going with the flow comes naturally to us – we are in a greater domain of awareness.

I would love to be in the flow a lot more. I can get into that space sometimes at work, but my general sense of wellbeing is not good.

Dr Barbara: By being more aware of the trains of thought you get sucked into, you will start to recognise the patterns. You will also find you are less reactive. In other words, in situations that might once have triggered you, you'll notice you have greater equanimity, more ability to simply notice and let be, to accept and move on. And as Christopher said, be generous with yourself. We are human. Be kind to yourself. Don't take things personally. The story of humankind is the story of mistakes and learning, failure and growth, collapse and reinvention.

Okay. There's a lot here for me to digest. I need to create a plan of action. Let's see: there's things to do, habits to develop, people to bring into my life, people to let go of, changes in my daily routine, and books to read. I feel really excited about what is possible. I need to really assimilate all this and make a plan.

Dr Barbara: That's a great idea. Start today. Don't overwhelm yourself. Things take time. If you can take one step each day in the new direction, you are doing really well. And remember, repetition is what builds your new, healthy habits so stick at it.

Where do you recommend I start?

Dr Barbara: What feels right for you? Trust yourself to know this. Listen to your inner wisdom. A big part of the recovery process is learning to trust yourself and know that you have the answers that are true for you. You can seek guidance and support for sure. But developing that self-trust will empower you to heal yourself. Then you will stand tall in your own shoes, knowing that you did it. With help, for sure, but it was you who brought yourself to health and fulfilment. It was you who made this conversation possible. It was you who asked the questions and created the space for this dialogue.

Thanks. I suppose I did.

Christopher: Once we've made a choice to expand our awareness, things tend to fall into place. We might be browsing online and a book randomly stands out and appeals to us. One day, we might be sitting in a coffee shop and a friend in recovery walks in and starts a conversation that expands our lives. I find it's best to stay open to what manifests in the present moment – to plan but welcome change as it arises.

I can see a day when I will be free of my addictions. I can see the day and get a sense of what my life will be like.

Dr Barbara: That's really great, and important. As Einstein said, things get created twice, once in the imagination and once in reality. Ask yourself, "What does it feel like to be healthy?" Create that feeling inside yourself. Create that reality. Imagine yourself going about your life, free to choose, grounded in yourself, clear in your relationships and in touch with your feelings. Build that sense of yourself from the inside. Know that it is possible. Actually, it seems to me it's becoming highly probable.

What else can I do? Any other suggestions?

Christopher: Pay attention to the good in your reality. Appreciate the abundance in your life – the simple things such as being able to breathe in fresh air, the smell of a sweet fragrance from a flower, tasting honey fresh from a honeycomb, enjoying the sunshine, taking a walk on the beach and being able to read or listen to these words. Or being able to connect with people on a deeper level – they are all things we can honour in our hearts.

I'm going to invest in a gratitude journal. It's so easy to forget what's good in my life. And I'm going to take action today!

Christopher: An appreciation for life will keep you grounded and in a rich state of plenty, rather than filled with want, scarcity and neediness. Remember that addiction is a perception of inner scarcity. We can transcend our deepest fears and addictions with an attitude of gratitude and by doing our best to treat others as we wish to be treated.

Hearing your stories has made that evident. I know now that addictions are not monsters – more like 'false friends', as you call them. I like that way of looking at it. It works for me. These false friends were essential but are no longer necessary. I feel that I can ac-

cept the things that don't work without judgement. There's a sense of space around it all instead of this feeling of dread and fear. I feel like it's possible to be kind to myself and start to really engage in life. Thank you both so much. I love sharing like this.

Dr Barbara: Thank you so much for your courage and openness. I feel inspired by you to live my life with greater courage and openness. I've learnt a great deal from this conversation. Thank you.

Christopher: Thank you for an enlightening and heartfelt conversation. It's been truly helpful and inspiring to learn from you both. Until next time, thank you.

About the authors

Both Christopher Dines and Dr Barbara Mariposa reside in the United Kingdom.

About Dr Barbara Mariposa

Dr Barbara Mariposa, MBBS, BSc, MFPHM (1), MICFEA

Dr Barbara is a medical doctor, thought leader and educator in the fields of health, emotional intelligence, mindfulness, and leadership. She specialises in the practices and scientific theories that bring together mind, emotion and body, in order to help people and organisations be healthy and successful. Among her main concerns are the high levels of hidden addiction in business, be it to substances such as cocaine, alcohol, and other so-called recreation drugs, or to excessive work, exercise, food and damaging relationships.

As a medical doctor, she specialised in psychiatry and holds a degree in psychology. She has extensive experience of addictions and their impact at both professional and personal levels. She sees addiction as a spectrum of behaviours, at the far end of which are those who get labelled as addicts. Dr Barbara firmly holds that a new approach to addiction is needed: one that humanises and de-stigmatises the underlying suffering that leads all people to seek false refuge in destructive patterns of behaviour.

Mental illness is the silent, hidden epidemic of our age, and Dr Barbara talks openly about her own journey to healing. She does this in the hope that it will make it possible for others to do so, and with the conviction that this is an essential step to creating a healthier world. Her experiences within the ancient wisdom traditions, which contain highly relevant depths of understanding about the human condition, inform her work.

Based on her wide-ranging experience, skills and expertise, she created the powerful and pioneering Mind Mood Mastery Programme. Her one-to-one work is grounded in mindfulness, counselling, coaching, five-element acupuncture and embodied personal development.

Her passion is to support people in fulfilling their true potential, to educate people on the latest advances in our understanding of how humans work, and exponentially improve the ways in which we connect, communicate and relate. She believes this will foster wellbeing and success at both organisational and personal levels, and will diminish the crippling burden of addictions today.

For more information on Dr Barbara, visit:
drbarbaramariposa.com

About Christopher Dines

Christopher Francis Dines (born August 19, 1983) is an English mindfulness teacher, trainer, writer and former house DJ/producer.

DJ, producer and promoter (1994 to 2006)

Having a deep love for music, Christopher left high school at fifteen to pursue a full-time career as an electronic house DJ. At fifteen, Christopher promoted two British national top-eleven UK garage bands, The Genius Cru and DJ Deekline in North West London, for two years. Having DJed at prestigious venues such as City Loud at Turnmills, Ministry of Sound, Defected In The House at Pacha, London Fashion Week, The Loft (Trouble Anderson's Loft) and Garage City, Christopher's DJing career took him to Asia, where he travelled extensively. This subsequently led him to remix and produce underground electronic dance music.

Throughout this thrilling experience, unfortunately, Christopher's drug-taking and party lifestyle spiralled out of control, which led to full-blown alcohol and cocaine addiction. After a dark rock bottom, Christopher cleaned up aged twenty-one (summer 2004) and began to do some soul-searching. This led to a deep exploration of the human mind and roads to emotional wellbeing and self-realisation. This has been accomplished through intense self-education and with the invaluable help and guidance of enlightened mentors.

In 2005, Christopher co-founded an underground deep house record label, SuCasa Beats. He was the head of A&R from 2005 to 2006. As the driving force behind the label, Dines signed Afro Medusa, Andy Daniel (Defected Records), Marlon D (Defected Records), Steal Vybe, and Pablo Martinez (King Street) and promoted the label at the legendary Plan B club in Brixton, London.

While remixing the national-chart hit band Afro Medusa, and artists such as Marlon D, Samba La Casa, Steal Vybe and Onxy (Soul2Soul), mindfulness was gradually becoming a subtle practice.

Teacher, trainer and writer (2006 to present)

Christopher 'retired' from the electronic dance music industry in June 2006 to give public talks on inspirational ideas and self-awareness, and to hold personal development and mindfulness workshops and courses. He trains employers, employees and self-referrals to amplify emotional intelligence, emotional resilience and mindfulness in the workplace.

He has led mindfulness meditation workshops for Public Health England (PHE Cambridge), the Mental Health Commission, The Recovery Evolution Festival (Suffolk), East Coast Recovery Drug and Alcohol Rehab, EMI Wealth London, wealth management and sales offices, and runs private Mindfulness Burnout Prevention (MBP) courses for professionals at Neal's Yard, Covent Garden and Chelsea, London.

Christopher is the author of Mindfulness Meditation: Bringing Mindfulness into Everyday Life, Manifest Your Bliss: A Spiritual Guide to Inner Peace, A Ticket to Prosperity: Spiritual Lessons for an Abundant Life (Revised Edition), The Mystery of Belief: How to Manifest Your Dreams, and Mindfulness Burnout Prevention: An 8-Week Course for Professionals.

For more information on Christopher, visit:
christopherdines.com